Reactive Programming with Node.js

Fernando Doglio

Apress®

Reactive Programming with Node.js

Fernando Doglio
La Paz, Uruguay

ISBN-13 (pbk): 978-1-4842-2151-8   ISBN-13 (electronic): 978-1-4842-2152-5
DOI 10.1007/978-1-4842-2152-5

Library of Congress Control Number: 2016961432

Managing Director: Welmoed Spahr
Acquisitions Editor: Louise Corrigan
Development Editor: Corbin Collins
Technical Reviewer: Phil Nash
Editorial Board: Steve Anglin, Pramila Balan, Laura Berendson, Aaron Black, Louise Corrigan, Jonathan Gennick, Todd Green, Robert Hutchinson, Celestin Suresh John, Nikhil Karkal, James Markham, Susan McDermott, Matthew Moodie, Natalie Pao, Gwenan Spearing
Coordinating Editor: Nancy Chen
Copy Editor: Angela Burkey
Compositor: SPi Global
Indexer: SPi Global
Artist: SPi Global

Distributed to the book trade worldwide by Springer Science+Business Media New York, 233 Spring Street, 6th Floor, New York, NY 10013. Phone 1-800-SPRINGER, fax (201) 348-4505, e-mail orders-ny@springer-sbm.com, or visit www.springer.com. Apress Media, LLC is a California LLC and the sole member (owner) is Springer Science + Business Media Finance Inc (SSBM Finance Inc). SSBM Finance Inc is a Delaware corporation.

For information on translations, please e-mail rights@apress.com, or visit www.apress.com.

Apress and friends of ED books may be purchased in bulk for academic, corporate, or promotional use. eBook versions and licenses are also available for most titles. For more information, reference our Special Bulk Sales–eBook Licensing web page at www.apress.com/bulk-sales.

Any source code or other supplementary materials referenced by the author in this text are available to readers at www.apress.com. For detailed information about how to locate your book's source code, go to www.apress.com/source-code/. Readers can also access source code at SpringerLink in the Supplementary Material section for each chapter.

Printed on acid-free paper

To my loving wife and kids, without whom this book would've never happened...
Thank you!

Contents at a Glance

Contents

About the Author

Fernando Doglio has been working as a Web Developer for the past 10 years. In that time, he's come to love the web, and has had the opportunity of working with most of the leading technologies at the time, suchs as PHP, Ruby on Rails, MySQL, Node. js, Angular.js, AJAX, REST APIs and others. For the past few years, he's also been working creating scalable architectures for big data platforms.

He can be contacted on twitter at: @deleteman123

When not programming, he can be seen spending time with his family.

About the Technical Reviewer

Phil Nash is a developer evangelist for Twilio serving developer communities in London and all over the world. He is a Ruby, JavaScript and Swift developer, Google Developer Expert, blogger, speaker and occasionally a brewer. He can be found hanging out at meetups and conferences, playing with new technologies and APIs or writing open source code.

Acknowledgments

I'd like to thank the amazing technical reviewer involved in the project, Phil Nash, whose great feedback was a crucial contribution to the making of this book.

I'd also like to thank the rest of the Apress editorial team, whose guidance helped me through the process of writing this book.

Introduction

Reactive programming is clearly a trend these days, a lot of front-end developers are starting to take it into account because the nature their work (event-based, javascript) lends well to it. A lot is being written about it on the web for that environment but, sadly, the back-end is not getting the same amount of attention.

Thanks to Node.js, we now have a very similar environment on the server side that can allow developers to think in terms of RP (or even Functional Reactive Programming) in the same manner that front-end developers think when using that technique on their day-to-day.

This book will be interesting to Node.js developers (or even other back-end developer) because it will provide them with a new and different way to solve the problems they have everyday.

So, sit back, relax, and enjoy the book!

CHAPTER 1

■ ■ ■

Reactive 101

The concept of reactive programming (RP) is one of those "old new concepts" that tend to fade out of style for a while and then resurface a few years later, when no one is looking. This behavior causes new generations of developers, specially the early-adopter kind, to initially see it as a revolutionary new thing that they need to use.

But the truth in this case is that the actual concept is not exactly new; in fact you'll see that it has been around for over 30 years.

In this chapter I introduce the concept of RP, talk about who created it and when, and describe the types of problems it tries to solve and the different types of styles there are. By the end, you'll have all the information you need to get you started in the reactive path.

Defining Reactive Programming

For me to be able to define RP I need something more than just Wikipedia's definition, I need to talk about when the term was initially mentioned, the type of problems it tries to solve, and the different types of RP styles there are.

The Origins of Reactive Programming

The concept of RP has been around since 1985. It was coined by David Harel and Amir Pnueli back then, in their paper titled "On the Development of Reactive Systems" (available at www.wisdom.weizmann. ac.il/~harel/SCANNED.PAPERS/ReactiveSystems.pdf). In it, the authors describe reactive systems as:

> *Reactive systems... are repeatedly prompted by the outside world and their role is to continuously respond to external inputs.*

Although their definition of reactive systems was never meant just for software projects, I'll keep the book focused on that, since it's what we're interested in. The same thing was done a few years later by Gerard Berry, who in 1989 expanded the concept of reactive systems on the software development context in his paper "Real Time Programming: Special Purpose or General Purpose Languages" (available at https://hal.archives-ouvertes.fr/inria-00075494/document):

Electronic supplementary material The online version of this chapter (doi:10.1007/978-1-4842-2152-5_1) contains supplementary material, which is available to authorized users.

It is convenient to distinguish roughly between three kinds of computer programs. Transformational programs compute results from a given set of inputs; typical examples are compilers or numerical computation programs. Interactive programs interact at their own speed with users or with other programs; from a user point of view a time-sharing system is interactive. Reactive programs also maintain a continuous interaction with their environment, but at a speed which is determined by the environment, not by the program itself. Interactive programs work at their own pace and mostly deal with communications, while reactive programs only work in response to external demands and mostly deal with accurate interrupt handling.

Real-time programs are usually reactive. However, there are reactive program that are not usually considered as being real-time, such as protocols, system drivers or man-machine interface handlers. All reactive programs require a common programming style.

Complex applications usually require establishing cooperation between the three kinds of programs. For example, a programmer uses a man-machine interface involving menus, scroll bars and other reactive devices. The reactive interface permits him to tell the interactive operating systems to start transformational computations such as program compilations.

To put it another way, RP describes a system that receives input from outside sources and is constantly processing them at the speed in which they come.

And from that, we can also gather that there is a very tight relationship between real-time projects and RP, so we will be keeping this in mind for future chapters when we start working on our own library.

Interestingly enough and to add a bit more to our History Channel moment, reactive systems are designed around dataflows, which is another old-but-goodie programming paradigm—in this case, from the 1960s. So let's quickly go into what dataflows are so we can have a better understanding of how reactive systems are built, shall we?

Dataflows 101

Just like RP, dataflow programming (created by Jack Dennis and his graduate students at MIT in the 60s) is another of the many programming paradigms out there. In this particular case, it works by modeling programs as directed graphs of data flowing between operations.

In this case, the nodes of the graph are the operations to be done over the data, and all they need to be executed is their input to be available. So in contrast with a more classic programming paradigm (like sequential or procedural programming), coming up with an architecture to do parallel processing is quite simple, because the only relevant information to the entire system is the available data (forget about keeping state, just worry about input and output data).

Dataflow programs or even dataflow architectures are very simple to scale out and grow when handling great amounts of information, especially compared to more traditional programs that tend to do everything at once instead of splitting the workload between processing units (nodes on the graph).

To put it simply, a dataflow language is one that handles the streams of information (data) and sends them from instruction to instruction, using flow control statements (like if statements) to control the actual flow of that stream.

Some examples of that are:

- Unix pipes (https://en.wikipedia.org/wiki/Pipeline_(Unix))

- LabVIEW (www.ni.com/labview/esa/)

- Ptolemy II (http://ptolemy.berkeley.edu/ptolemyII/)

- Shake (https://en.wikipedia.org/wiki/Shake_(software))

- And many more…

■ **Note**   This is but a simple introduction to the topic of dataflows. If you're interested in knowing more about the subject, I suggest you find a more specific book about it, such as *Dataflow and Reactive Programming Systems: A Practical Guide* by Matt Carkci (you can find it on Amazon by searching for its name).

How Dataflows and Reactive Programming Are Related

As we've seen, dataflows dictate that information can flow from node to node, where each node is an operation done on the data transmitted. This flow is one-way, in the sense that once the piece of data reaches the end node, the process is done. It can start again with another piece of data, but that's not strictly required.

Reactive programming, on the other hand, could be thought of as dataflows on steroids, for the following reasons:

- With RP we gain the concept of event streams, a source of continuous data where we can subscribe as the source for our operations.

- Because we now have the streams, we can also apply transformations to these streams, essentially creating new ones from the original one.

- One specific transformation we can apply to them, is the merge of several streams, a powerful operation that allows us to work with several streams at once.

- So basically, one can say that a dataflow routine is what happens to one particular piece of information that comes through one event stream.

In order to make the point completely clear, please look at Figure 1-1, which shows how a simple case of two variables being added can be incorporated into a reactive diagram with two continuous streams of numbers.

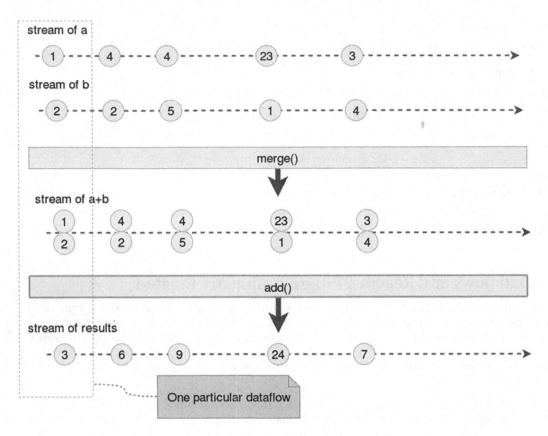

Figure 1-1. *Marble diagram showing the addition of values from two different streams*

Figure 1-1 shows each event on each stream as a circle, then a merge operation being done on both streams to create a new one, with a pair of numbers on each event. Finally, we add both numbers to return only one to yet, another stream. The horizontal lines represent time, and you can clearly see where the dataflow diagram fits into this one, basically cutting vertically through all layers of the reactive diagram.

■ **Note**　This particular example makes the assumption that all events on both streams will be added at exactly the same time, thus simplifying the merging task.

What Is RP Good For?

The classic example everyone gives when they're trying to explain how a reactive system works is that of a spreadsheet. Current spreadsheet software, like that of Google Docs, Microsoft Excel, or LibreOffice, all provide the ability to create formulas that depend on the values of certain cells, something like this:

```
=sum(A1:A20)
```

The code is very simple to understand, it will execute the mathematical sum of all values from cell A1 to, and including, the value of A20. Now the neat thing about this formula is not its result but the fact that we're referencing the actual cells involved in the calculation and not only their values. This effectively means that we can affect the content of those cells and the final result will be updated accordingly. Just like magic, only not.

Now let's extrapolate that concept and apply it to our day-to-day programming language of choice. I'm not going to focus on the paradigm we're using just now—it's not important at the moment. Now let's say we have some Node.js code. If you could subscribe to what happens to a particular variable, something like the following:

```
var myVariable = "initial value";
myVariable.onchange(function(new_vaule) {
    //... act accordingly
});
```

Just think how simple your code would become if you had the ability to do that instead of needing to monitor the value of the variable for any change and manually executing the registered callback functions.

Now let's take the previous example one step further. Let's think of any change to a specific variable as an event, and let's consider for a second that any response from an asynchronous service call is a change on the receiving variable (meaning on the variable you save the asynch response to), which would turn that response into an event as well. We can register to those event streams and react when new data are available.

For front-end programmers, this paradigm is probably very familiar, since they normally handle that type of mechanics when registering mouse-related event handlers (just to name one example). But that's already built into the DOM; the beauty of this is that we can do it for any type for service. For API calls, for instance, we can register one or more callbacks and just let them handle the responses when they start getting back to us.

The same goes to back-end developers, even though Node developers aren't that used to working with events (they have them, they're just not that common on the back-end, that's all), turning every database connection and every file read event into a source for an event stream could definitely simplify the code and the way we handle things like errors.

But wait! There is more! One more actually. With the aforementioned characteristics, reactive libraries all over are implementing transformations over the events on the streams, while at the same time treating these events as immutable entities. What this effectively means is that we can create new streams of events by mixing and chaining these transformations.

Let's look at a basic example. Consider the front-end comment from earlier. Streams of click events are probably one of the most common ones you'll find there. Now, what if you wanted to just capture the left-click events but also keep the full list of click events available for other parts of our code? Easy peasy, as Figure 1-2 shows.

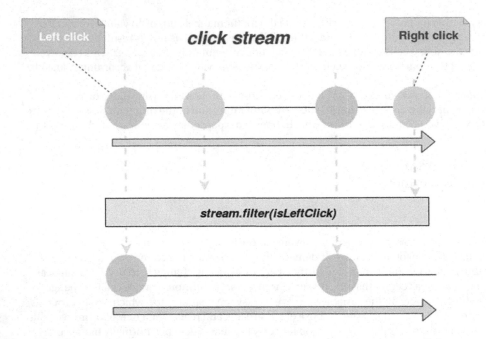

Figure 1-2. Sample marble diagram showing a filtering operation over mouse clicks

The diagram shows how new events appear on the stream as time moves forward (horizontal lines) and the operation being done over the initial stream (filter) in order to create a new one.

Let's take a more complex example. Say you have two buttons, Add and Subtract, and you want your code to add 1 to a counter every time you click the Add button, and to subtract 1 from the same counter every time you click Subtract. Figure 1-3 illustrates this.

Figure 1-3 translates actual events to just a stream of numbers (1 or –1) and then we merge them, creating a new one. Each value returned by this new "counter" stream will be handled by a function that will simply add the returned value to the current counter shown on screen. Simple, yet powerful.

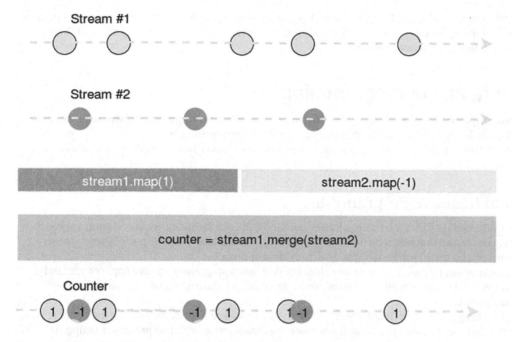

Figure 1-3. *Marble diagram showing a merge operation between two streams*

So basically, to sum things up and answer the original question in a more concise way, RP allows you, the developer, to handle streams of asynchronous events with ease and transform them into new streams It is a paradigm that can be applied both for the back-end as well as for the front-end.

Reactive vs. Observer Pattern

With everything talked about so far, you might say that RP is just an implementation of the observer pattern and that by using that, you would get the same results.

Not quite. Consider for a moment that I'm not really focusing on JavaScript just yet, or any language for that matter, so first off, you can't really think in object-oriented programming (OOP) terms when some languages don't even speak it (you might accomplish something similar without OOP, mind you, but that's outside the point). And even if they do, conceptually they're similar but not the same. Check out Table 1-1 for a quick look.

Table 1-1. *Comparison of the Observer Pattern vs. the RP Paradigm*

Observer Pattern	Reactive Programming
Meant to report state to registered observers.	When the value of a variable changes, all other values that depend on it will consequently get updated.
Works on whole objects.	Level of granularity reaches the single primitive variable.
Offers direct communication between observed objects and observers. In other words, the state of the observed object is transmitted without any change.	Transformations can be applied to each transmitted event, creating new ones on the way.

If you want, you can think of RP as going one step further from a simple observer implementation, since you're not just notifying the interested observer, you're also automatically reacting (see what I did there?) accordingly by updating the related elements.

Types of Reactive Programming

There are several approaches to RP. They mainly depend on the programming language you're using, and they all get the job done, so picking the right one, is purely a preference thing.

This section looks at the three most common approaches these days: functional, object-oriented, and declarative.

Functional Reactive Programming

Next to object-oriented RP (discussed soon), functional RP (FRP) is probably the most common approach currently being used. And that might be because the concepts already discussed (especially how stream transformations can be done) can be mapped to a functional approach.

To be more specific, FRP uses the building blocks of *functional programming* (like map, reduce, and filter) to process and transform the streams of events generated by the asynchronous sources that we might be dealing with.

Future chapters go into more detail about FRP. Here I'll just look at a quick example of the benefits you can get from this approach. Think of a generic microservice architecture, with two particular endpoints:

```
/users #will return the list of users on the system, but with minimum data
(only id and full name)

/users/:id #will return the details of a particular user, which could imply things like id,
full name, date of birth, address and telephone number.
```

Granted that this definition might not be the smartest API design, but let's go with it for the purpose of this example. What I want from this is the list of users, but with full details on each of them.

Now a traditional Node.js approach, would be to do something like:

```
request('/users', function(users) {
    async.map(users, function(user, done) {
        request('/users/' + user.id, function(userData){
            console.log("User data obtained for user: ",  user.id);
            done(null, userData);
        }, function(fullUsers) {
            //return the list to the client
        });
    }
});
```

Nothing wrong with the preceding code, actually, and that is in part because I'm using the async library (available at http://caolan.github.io/async/). Without it, the iteration between users to request their full data would've meant quite a lot more lines of code and, even worse, more logic thrown into the mix. And this is key to why FRP is so great—the focus of the developer should be on solving the problem at hand (in this case, getting a list of full user objects) and not on how to solve the problems presented by the technology used (in this case, we're referring to the asynchronicity of the requests).

Again, there is nothing wrong with the preceding code, but look at Figure 1-4.

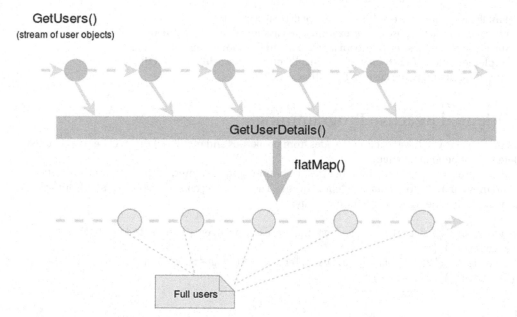

GetUsers()
(stream of user objects)

Figure 1-4. *Marble diagram with the RP approach of the current example*

And now look at the following code:

```
GetUsers()
    .map(function(u) {
        return '/users/' + u.id;
    })
    .pipe(getUserDetails)
    .flatMap();
```

■ **Note**   The preceding code is not referencing any specific reactive library for Node.js. Its purpose is to show the reader the simplifications that come from using this approach.

Granted, the code is also simplified because we're not directly calling the request function, but it is also much easier to read and simpler to understand. The indentation level of the callbacks is kept in check, even if we were to add an extra step in the flow.

Here's what's happening in the preceding code, step-by-step:

1. Generate a stream of users, by making the request and then returning the stream of users back.

2. We're applying one transformation to the stream, generating urls for each user's details endpoint based on the user objects.

3. Each url is piped to the getUserDetails function, which will in turn request the data from that URL and return the information. This operation can be done asynchronously without any added complexity, but the order of the users will be lost.

4. Finally, we flatten the resulting stream of lists, and get a stream of full user objects. For the purpose of this example, just assume that `flatMap` also turns the resulting stream into an actual list, but that would depend on the implementation of `flatMap` you're using, I'll go into more detail about that once I start implementing the custom FRP library.

Object-Oriented Reactive Programming

OORP states that objects will have reactions (asides from properties and methods) that will be re-evaluated when the data they depend on changes.

Let's look at the example I talked about before, two buttons and a counter; in this example, the buttons are objects and they can react to events, like "click" events. The following code uses the popular front-end library jQuery to provide the basic OORP functionality:

```
//Sets the value of the "counter" based on the streams of events generated by both buttons
function setCounter() {
        var value = $("#add").data('values').length - $("#substract").data('values').length;
        $("#counter").text(value);
}

$("#substract").click(function() {
        var stream = $(this).data('values')
        stream.push(1);
        $(this).data('values', stream);
        setCounter();
});

$("#add").click(function() {
        var stream = $(this).data('values')
        stream.push(1);
        $(this).data('values', stream);
        setCounter();
});
```

■ **Note**   The preceding example clearly lacks all the boilerplate code needed to import the library, set up the initial state, and so on. That is not needed to make the point of OORP.

In the example code, you can clearly see that the #counter element's value depends directly on the values added to the streams represented by the arrays on the #add button and the #substract one. The setCounter function takes care of ensuring that relationship.

The language I'm using for the example is JavaScript, and because it isn't purely reactive, I have to manually handle some of the magic. In this case, the update on the final value depending on the streams has to be done manually. That being said, on the other hand, the reaction re-evaluation is done automatically by the system when a click event occurs, and that is completely done for us.

Declarative Reactive Programming

DRP is an alternative paradigm to what we've already covered. It is based, no surprise here, on the declarative programming paradigm, which states that the developer focuses on *declaring* what the program is meant to be doing, instead of *how* it is supposed to do it.

Table 1-2 shows an example of DRP.

Table 1-2. *Small Comparison of Declarative Code vs. Classic Imperative Code*

Declarative Code	Imperative Code

```var numbers = [1,2,3,4,5,6,7,8,9,0];```
 	
```var odds = _.filter(numbers, (n) =>```
```{ return n % 2 === 0; });```
	```var numbers = [1,2,3,4,5,6,7,8,9,0];```
	
	```var odds = [];```
	
	```numbers.forEach(function(n) {```
	`    if(n % 2 === 0) {`
	`        odds.push(n);`
	`    }`
	```});```

In Prolog:
 	
```likes(mike, food)```
```likes(mike, tv)```
```likes(michelle, food)```
 	
```?- likes(michelle, tv)```
```no.```
	I don't even want to think about it.

Clearly the declarative code is much simpler to understand at first sight: far fewer lines of code to read and a lot less logic to comprehend. Other examples of declarative languages are Prolog, CSS (although not a *programming* language, it's still declarative), and even SQL. When it comes to DRP, one might consider the preceding and say that this is the purest reactive approach among them all.

On a declarative language, you would only have to define the logic rules that define your program and then the compiler would take care of the rest. In other words, you can specify how different variables and objects depend on each other simply by declaring that relationship, and the system will take care of watching over changes and notifying the interested parties.

Reactive Programming vs. Traditional Programming

By this time, I've covered the origins of RP, the main types of RP, and what it is good for, so you should have a pretty good idea of what are the main differences between RP and the classic programming paradigms, like imperative and OOP.

That being said, Table 1-3 covers those differences in case they're not so clear right now.

Table 1-3. *Comparison of RP vs. Traditional Programming*

Reactive Programming	Traditional Model
The level of abstraction of your code is high, allowing you to focus on core business rules.	Lower level of abstraction, because you also have to deal with the technology's intricacies.
Usually, lower development times, since you're only focusing on the problem to solve, which translates into fewer lines of code.	Usually, higher development times, because you also have to workaround the limitations of the chosen technology, which in turn translates into more lines of code needed.
Writes code describing the *what to do* instead of the *how to do it.* This simplifies the code and makes maintenance much easier.	Writes code describing *how to do it* instead of *what to do.* This adds extra complexity to your code.
Values that depend on others are updated automatically without the need to use any logic. In the following line, the value of A gets updated whenever B or C changes. A := B + C	Values do not depend on each other dynamically. In the following line, the value of A is not changed unless manually updated by the developer. A = B + C

■ **Tip** Think of RP vs. Non-RP as the difference between using a car to go to your work everyday and building that car from spare parts before you can actually use it.

Summary

This first chapter covered a basic introduction to reactive programming. It discussed how it originated, the different types there are, and what good it is. It compared reactive vs. non-reactive programming to better understand its benefits.

In the next chapter, we'll continue covering the basics of RP, although this time, I talk about the way the developer needs to *think* of reactive systems when developing them.

CHAPTER 2

■ ■ ■

Being Reactive

Now that I've established what reactive programming (RP) is, and why you would want to use it, the next logical step would be to start thinking about adjusting your mindset in order to *properly* use it. Since I'm dealing with a new paradigm here, you can't just tackle this problem with an OOP mindset, or a functional mindset and solve it in a reactive kind of way, you need to start thinking reactively.

So, in this chapter I will do just that: I'll basically try to show you how to think in a reactive way. And to accomplish that, I will:

- Show you some problem solving techniques for Node.js and where they fall short.

- Solve those shortcomings with RP.

By the end of this chapter, you'll know how to get into a reactive mindset.

Keep in mind though that the RP examples provided in this chapter will not refer to a specific library just yet, they will be pseudo-code examples that look a lot like JavaScript. Once you reach Chapter 6, you'll be able to pick one specific library and write the examples using that one.

But First, a Word About Marbles

Or, moreso, on marble diagrams. I have used them in Chapter 1 and did not really explain them, but since I'm now about to show you several of them, with increasing levels of complexity, I might as well go over the basics of what a marble diagram is and how it can help you better understand reactive data flows.

Marble diagrams are a way to visually represent reactive data streams.

What that quote basically means is that with marble diagrams, you have a set of tools that allow you to represent the transformations that a data stream goes through during a reactive data flow.

In particular, I'm going to show you a small variation of marble diagrams that I'll be using throughout the entire book; the basic ideas are there, but I'll also add a few extra standards to better explain the behavior I'm trying to display. So without further ado, let's take a look at Figure 2-1, which shows the basic structure of a simple diagram.

© Fernando Doglio 2016

F. Doglio, *Reactive Programming with Node.js*, DOI 10.1007/978-1-4842-2152-5_2

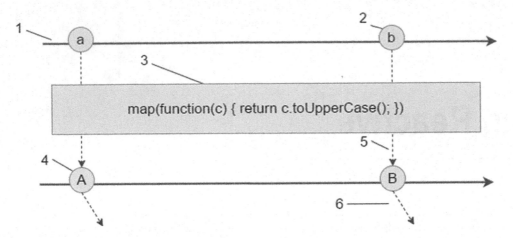

Figure 2-1. *Basic structure of a marble diagram*

It's not that hard to understand how the dataflows and which operations are being done over it. Here's what each number in the figure represents:

1. Horizontal lines, going from left to right, represent time.

2. The circles on top of the horizontal lines are the events generated by the stream.

3. The big box on the center of the diagram represents the operations being performed on the stream.

4. The marbles below the previously mentioned box, are the results of applying the operation on the box to each event from the stream.

5. Vertical dotted lines represent the life span of one marble.

6. Finally, inclined dotted lines represent an external service call being done.

The flow shown in Figure 2-1 is very simple, it just turns every character of the stream to its uppercase version, but doing something more complex is, nevertheless, just as simple. Say you wanted to merge two streams of numbers and then get the highest of them all, you can easily do that with the diagram from Figure 2-2.

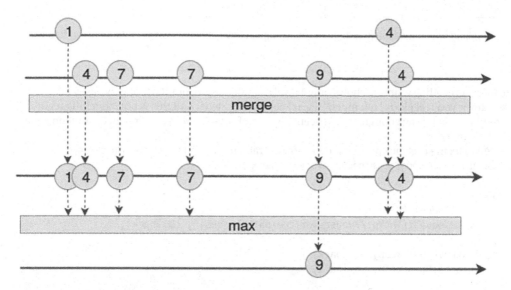

Figure 2-2. *Marble diagram showing a more complex operation*

Lots of marbles in Figure 2-2, I know, but look past them and you'll see two simple steps: *merge* and *max*—that's it. The only relevant thing to note here would be that the max function would only emit one value, and it would do so after both original streams had ended. Now that this is out of the way, let's move on to this chapter's intended content, shall we?

Moving Away from Traditional Techniques

In this section I'll look at different common "problems" the standard Node.js developer needs to solve in his/her day-to-day job and the standard solution for each one. In turn, I'll analyze that solution and you'll end up seeing if a reactive approach would've been a better idea.

Example #1 – Your Run-of-the-Mill Callback Hell

There is nothing particularly new about this problem—we've all faced it at one point or another: the moment when you have to execute a series of functions on a preset order, as a series of steps, if you will:

```
makeRequest("http://yourserver.com/path/request", function step1(req, resp) {
        processData(resp, function step2(err, processedData) {
                saveData(processedData, function step3(err, model) {
                        loadRelatedData(model, function step4(err, relData) {
                                model.rel = relData;
                                sendResponse(model);
                        });
                });
        });
});
```

■ **Note** Error handling was intentionally left out of the example above, since it doesn't add anything to the point of callback hell.

The code in the preceding example shows only 4 levels of indentation, but it could very easily be increased to whatever you feel like is "too much" if you keep adding steps. And this is not stretching reality. If you've been around Node.js long enough, you've seen this type of code; either you wrote it, or someone you work with wrote it, but it's real.

If you wanted to fix the previous problem, there are several options, you could go with the async.js module (available from www.npmjs.com/package/async), like so:

```
async.waterfall([
        function(callback) {
                makeRequest("http://youserver.com/path/request", callback);
        },
        function step1(req, resp, callback) {
                processData(resp, callback);
        },
        function step2(err, processedData, callback) {
                saveData(processedData, callback);
        },
        function step3(err, model, callback) {
                loadRelatedData(model, callback);
        },
        function step4(err, relData, callback) {
                model.rel = relData;
                callback(null, model);
        }
], function(err, model) {
        sendResponse(model);
});
```

The resulting code has successfully reduced the indentation level, but the number of lines has, unfortunately, increased. This makes reading and understanding it not necessarily easier, because you now have to mentally parse the unfamiliar structure provided by the waterfall method.

A promises approach would help a bit, thanks to the simpler syntax provided by Promises but having to manually deal with the intricacies of promises (every step of the process would need to return a new promise object, you would also have to wrap your asynch functions to so use them as promises, and so on) would harm the readability of the code.

You need a solution that deals with a promise-like approach but abstracts the developers from that same mechanics; in other words, you should not be thinking about the tool you are using, only on how best to use it. You need something like this:

```
makeRequest("http://yourserver.com/path/request")
        .pipe(step1)
        .pipe(step2)
        .pipe(step3)
        .pipe(step4)
```

Yes, the waterfall code can be made to look a lot like the preceding example if you create the functions somewhere else and then simply pass in their reference. But this is not just about lines of code, it's also about readability and semantics. The new example has no waterfall on it, it simply lets you pipe your content from one function to the next; you don't need to think about promises or how the data is sent from one step to the next. You simply know it's happening—that's what I'm looking for and that's what you should also aim for.

Let's keep this basic example in mind for now and move forward into more complex issues, it will all start to look better in a bit.

Example #2 – Nested Asynchronous Calls

Chapter 1 sort of covered this one briefly, but let's go over it once again, with more details.

The basic premise of this example is that you have an external service request (be it an http request, a socket call, a database query, whatever) that returns a number of results, and for each result, you want to do a series of external service requests. Basically, this example is similar to the previous one, but instead of one request after another, in here you have a bunch of asynchronous calls being done in parallel. As we all know, in Node.js this means we're diving into asynchronicity hell, where every call needs to be done before moving into the next item, but every item is doing things asynchronously, so they're all queuing up. How do we handle this?

```
getUsers(function(usrs) {
        var fullUsrs = [];
        var total = usrs.length;

        if(total == 0) return;

        usrs.forEach(function(usr) {
                if(usr.age > 18) {
                        loadExtraData(usr, function(err, fullUsr) {
                                getFriends(fullUsr, function(err, friends) {
                                        fullUsr.friends = friends;
                                        fullUsrs.push(fullUsr)
                                        displayUser(fullUsr);
                                })
                        })
                }
        })
})
```

Take a look at the preceding code; as usual, the easy functions are left out due to simplicity reasons. There are three functions that do some sort of external service query (getUsers, loadExtraData, and getFriends), out of which the first is the simplest one, because it has no context—it just queries a services and returns the list of objects. The other two though, they need to be called once for each object, and since they're both asynchronous, you need to handle that part as well. It's also only displaying the information for the users who are older than 18 years, so there is a filter there as well; you need to remember that.

With that being said, let's try to map everything the function was doing on the previous code into Figure 2-3, which exemplifies how this example is resolved using RP.

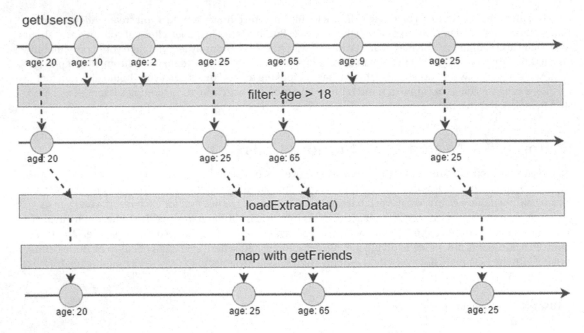

Figure 2-3. *Marble diagram showing an RP approach to the problem at hand*

In Figure 2-3 you see every major step from the code example, without having to mentally parse the code:

- The initial stream of users, returned by the getUsers function

- The filtering of those items by age

- An asynchronous call for every item that passed the filter (from the loadExtraData function call)

- The map step has an asynchronous call for every item and a modification to that item as well. This is the last transformation step.

If you go back to the functional reactive way of writing code, you can probably do something like the following:

```
getUsers()
        .filter(function(usr) { return usr.age > 18 })
        .pipe(loadExtraData)
        .map(getFriends(function(usr, friends) {
                usr.friends = friends;
                return usr;
        }))
        .pipe(displayUser)
```

This code is just like Figure 2-3, one level above the abstraction level we usually think on, because it's not focusing on edge cases, or *forEach* blocks or asynchronous behavior at all; instead it's focusing on the overall task at hand and the four steps we described on the diagram.

Example #3 – Handling Throttleable Input Streams

This is not a simple pattern that can be replaced like with the first two examples; this example deals with the case where you have an input stream with events that happen too fast and need to be throttled.

To make matters more specific and provide a better example, let's write down a use case for a fictional app:

- You want your application to let the user input a word or a phrase and, while the user is still typing, lookup a translation for that string.

- You'll want this application to be a command line Node.js application.

- Because you're hitting an external service to provide the translation, you'll also want to handle retries in case the communication to that service fails.

With that in mind, here is what that code would look like, using traditional imperative, non-reactive programming:

```
var stdin = process.stdin;

stdin.setRawMode(true);
stdin.resume();

var currentWord = '';
var retries = 0;
stdin.on('data', function(input) {
        input = input.toString();
        currentWord += input;

        console.log(currentWord) //Show the input to the user

        if(input.charCodeAt(0) === 27) process.exit(0); //exit with ESC
        if(input.charCodeAt(0) === 13) { //start a new input string with ENTER
                currentWord = "";
                console.log(" ");
        }

        if(currentWord.length > 0) {
                getTranslation(currentWord, retries, callback);
        }
})

/**
The callback that handles the translation response
@err is the error message, or null if there is no error
@trans is the translation string
@attempt is the current attempt being made
@string is the string that you're trying to translate
*/
function callback(err, trans, attempt, string) {
        if(err) {
                console.error(err, " - retries: ", attempt);
                if(attempt < 3) {
                        return getTranslation(string, attempt + 1, callback);
```

```
                } else {
                        retries = 0;
                        return console.log("Fatal error, retrying is not helping: ", err)
                }
        }
        console.log("'",trans,"'")
}

//Fake translation service below
var __DICT__ = {
        "hello": "Hola",
        "yes": "Sí",
        "no": "No",
        "i": "Yo",
        "i do not understand":"Yo no comprendo",
        "who": "Quién",
        "why": "Por qué",
        "test": "prueba",
        "who are you": "Quién eres"
};

function getTranslation(word, retry, cb) {
        //simulate a service call by sleeping for a few seconds
        var high = 5
        var low = 1;
        var sleepTime = Math.random() * (high - low) + low;

        word = word.toLowerCase();

        setTimeout(function() {
                var translation = null;
                if( translation = __DICT__[word]) {
                        return cb(null, translation, retry, word);
                } else {
                        return cb("No translation found for: " + word, null, retry, word);
                }
        }, sleepTime * 1000)
}
```

▦ **Note** As you can see, I'm actually faking the external service call, but for the purpose of this example, the simplicity of the code will help us keep our focus where it should go.

Right off the bat, there are a couple of problems to be solved that I can think of by looking at that code:

- Because the app won't wait until the ENTER key is pressed, you'll need to react on every keystroke, and therefore, you'll want to avoid trying to translate the unfinished word or phrase. So you'll have to deal with this somehow.

- Due to the continuous input and the asynchronous nature of the external service calls, you might run into a timing issue. If the system is able to translate part of your phrase while you're typing it and that response arrives AFTER the final phrase's translation does, you can end up with the wrong result.

Now, even though the above code clearly works to an extent, like you've already seen, some quirks have not been handled. This is not to say it can't be fixed, but doing so would take a lot more work and code than what I'm willing to put into this example, especially because in a minute, I'll provide a solution to it that requires you to write less code.

So, let's take a look at Figure 2-4, and then I'll code it using a functional reactive pseudo-code.

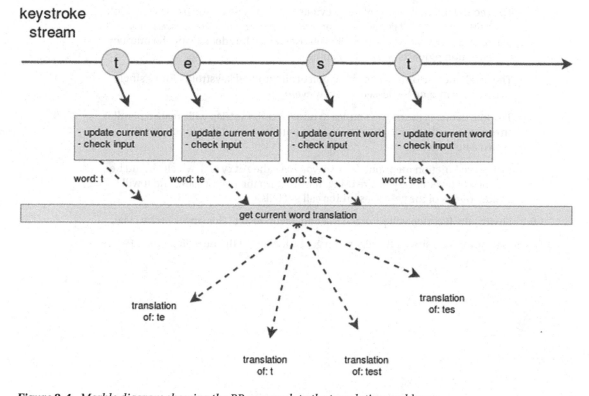

Figure 2-4. *Marble diagram showing the RP approach to the translation problema*

In Figure 2-4, you can see the problems we mentioned earlier:

- Continuous requests for the translation service

- Out-of-order responses due to possible delays on the translation services

How can you fix those problems? Very simple, using a functional RP approach, you can transform the initial keystrokes stream into something easier to handle, and from there, you can keep transforming the stream into something you can translate. Let's look at the code:

```
readInput()
        . throttle(300)
        .scan('', '.concat')
```

```
    .flatMapLatest(function(word) {
        return retry(getTranslation(word), 3);
    })
    .pipe(printTranslation)
```

It's still not using any library so the code is kept generic, I'll get to that eventually, don't worry. Although the code should be easy to understand, some of the names are not helping, so let's quickly go over the six lines above:

1. This one is pretty clear. It reads the standard input and creates a stream with the keystrokes.

2. The second one solves one of the previous problems: Reacting to every keystroke, by throttling the event generation from the source stream, you're essentially reacting to bursts of events every 300 milliseconds, thus decreasing the number of translation requests you end up doing.

3. The third one performs a concatenation of all throttled keystrokes into a single string that can then be passed as a new event.

4. The fourth one is the most complex to understand. flatMap will create a parallel stream to handle the function passed as a parameter, and that function will return a new stream.

5. Inside the function mentioned above, you have the retry call, which should be part of whatever library you're using. It will return the new stream, and it will handle retries of the getTranslation call if it fails.

6. Finally, the last step will print out the translation result. This one is pretty clear.

You can see how much simple the algorithm got by looking at the new diagram in Figure 2-5.

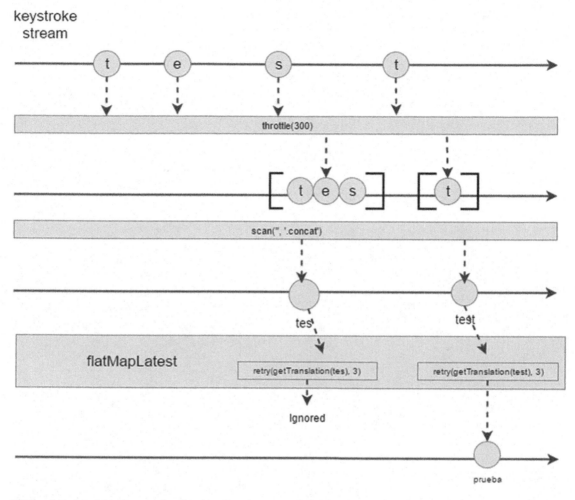

Figure 2-5. *Marble diagram for the new RP solution with throttle*

A quick look at the diagram shows very graphically what happens to the keystrokes throughout the entire dataflow proposed previously. In the end, and obviously assuming the throttling step divides the input into two, you end up with only two calls to the translation service instead of the four that would've taken place using the original code, and thanks to the `flatMapLatest` function, only the result of the second translate call is accepted.

It is true that what was achieved here could've been done using classical imperative programming, but the extra effort and extra lines of code are not really worth it if you compare it to this functional reactive approach.

Summary

This chapter covered some of the most common cases that you might be interested in solving using RP. You saw how they're handled by regular imperative programming, how complicated they are to solve if you take into account every edge case, and, finally, how much simpler they are if you approach them with RP.

Chapter 3 will start getting deeper into *Functional* Reactive Programming. I'll cover the basics of Functional Programming in Node.js and then you'll see how that applies to RP (I've already showed some examples of that, but this time, I'll get into more details).

CHAPTER 3

■ ■ ■

Functional Reactive Programming

In the previous chapters I've tried to keep the code examples as independent of everything else as possible (especially the reactive code examples), which is why I haven't mentioned any particular library just yet, and that is why you can't just copy and paste some of it and just run it.

One of the main things to note about the previous chapters is that most of the reactive examples were made using concepts of functional programming (map, passing functions as variables, etc.) so it should not be a surprise for you that the topic of this chapter is, indeed, functional reactive programming.

In this chapter, you'll start getting closer to the actual act of coding working code (hooray!) and you'll do that by tackling the following topics:

- An introduction to functional programming (FP) in JavaScript. Here I'll go over the relevant bits of FP. I'll try to go over them quickly and show some code examples to help explain how they work internally and how they can help us on our tasks.

- The main tools of a functional programmer. Related to the previous point, I'll cover the three main tools any functional programmer should learn to love, map, reduce and filter.

- How to deal with observable streams of events.

An Intro to Functional Programming in JavaScript

The topic of FP in JavaScript is, to be honest, a topic in and of itself, and I could easily write an entire book about it. That being said, I'll try to summarize that topic here, in one chapter. The chapter will cover the most important parts about FP, leaving the heavy theory mostly out. If, by the end of this chapter, you're left wanting to learn more about this subject, please go and get one of those books (like *Becoming Functional* by Joshua Backfield or *Functional Thinking* by Neal Ford), they're definitely worth it

With that out of the way, let's begin by defining some concepts that will be used throughout this chapter: pure functions, composition, currying, and monads.

■ **Remember**   The following explanation will be done in the context of JavaScript, so if you're already familiar with a more generic version of these concepts, bear in mind I'm limiting the explanation to keep things simple and easy to understand.

© Fernando Doglio 2016

F. Doglio, *Reactive Programming with Node.js*, DOI 10.1007/978-1-4842-2152-5_3

Pure Functions

In FP, there is this concept of *pure functions,* which might strike you as a weird thing to define, considering you've being dealing with functions (or methods) basically your entire development life (if you haven't, I just don't know what kind of strange language you've been programming on).

So what does it take for a function to be *pure* then? A pure function must comply with the following two statements:

- It cannot have unforeseen side effects when executed. In other words, a function must return the exact same result every time it is called with the same parameters.

- It can only depend on the parameters it receives for its internal logic. Meaning that even when there is no side effect from its execution, it can't depend on external values to perform its calculations because those values might change, thus affecting the function's result, which in turn goes against the previous point.

Table 3-1 shows a quick example.

Table 3-1. *Examples of Pure and Impure Functions*

Pure Function	Impure Function
```function pure(a, b, c, d) { return a + b + c + d; }```	```var sum = 0; function impure(a,b,c,d) { sum = a + b + c; //modifies an external variable return a + b + c + d; }```
```function pure(a, b) { var mult = 2; return (a+b) * mult; }```	```var mult = 2; function impure(a, b) { return (a+b) * mult; }```

The examples in Table 3-1 clearly show the unwanted side effect of the *impure function* on the first row and the unwanted external dependency on the second row. In both cases, the execution of the *impure* functions would yield unwanted results.

The concept of *pure functions* is fairly simple, yet crucial to the implementation of functional programming, so it is important that you understand it completely. As an additional note, even though this is not directly related to FP, having *pure functions* as part of your code simplifies the cognitive load on the developers using or reading your code, since the effort to understand the logic inside your functions is now considerably lower. Another benefit of this type of functions is that they're much easier to test since they only rely on their input values.

Composition

Function composition is another big pillar of functional programming, because along with *pure functions* it provides us, the developers, the means to create complex constructs that stay true to the constraints imposed by the paradigm.

From a mathematical point of view, function composition looks like this:

```
compose(f(x), g(x)) = f(g(x))
```

Now, if you translate that into JavaScript, composing functions looks like this:

```
var add10 = function(a) { return a + 10; };
var double = function(b) { return b * 2; };

var addAndDouble = compose(add10, double); //add10(double(a));
addAndDouble(10); //returns 40;
```

This example shows a very basic composition, and even though it does help explain the basic behavior of this operation, let's look at a more complex example to better understand how much use we can get out of it.

For this, let's assume you are working on a TO-DO list application, which, let's face it, is the new *Hello World* of the programming world. In this application, we want to get a list of all the completed tasks, so using pure JavaScript, you'd write the following:

```
var doneTasks = tasks.filter(function(t) { return t.done; });
```

You could say that that's a functional approach; after all you're passing in a *pure* function as filter, and it works. But we can do one better:

```
var doneTasks = filter(where({done: true}));
```

No I didn't forget about the *tasks* list, in the example the *doneTasks* variable contains a function and not the actual list of filtered tasks, and that function would filter whatever list of tasks we pass it as parameter when executed. So we have re-usability (yay!). I know I just came up with two new functions and I'm not really explaining how they work, but there is a reason for that: I'm not done discussing the tools you need to create them. Once you've finished reading this section of the chapter, you should have all you need to create them yourself.

That being said, there is another upside to the new approach: the ability to compose, say you also want to group that list by user. You can group the tasks using a given `partition` function, it would work just like `compose`, but using the `Array.prototype.reduce` method, it would create a dictionary of elements indexed by the attribute you want.

```
var groupByUser = partition({prop: 'username'});
var groupedTasks = compose(groupByUser, doneTasks);
```

And now, using two simple functions, you created a third, more complex one that remains *pure*. Even though the *compose* function is quite simple to understand, let me show you an implementation for both, partition and compose:

```
function partition(byProp, list) {
    return list.reduce(function(dict, curr) {
        var idxValue = dict[byProp.prop]; //use the property we passed as parameter
        if( !dict[idxValue] ) dict[idxValue] = []; //initial value
        dict[idxValue].push(curr);
        return dict;
    },{});
}
function compose(fn1, fn2) {
    return function() {
        return fn1(fn2.call(fn2, arguments));
    }
}
```

The function is not really that complex now that you have had a look at it; all it has to do is understand how the *reduce* function works, which, simply put, allows you to iterate over the values of the array and apply a function to it that will reduce all values to only one. The other interesting thing about the above code is that it receives *two* parameters, but on the example I'm only passed one, so what gives?!

This is a perfect time to start talking about *currying* functions, so let's!

Currying Functions

Try to ignore the sudden crave for Indian food you have right now (https://en.wikipedia.org/wiki/Curry), because this has nothing to do with it (in fact, it's related to Haskell Curry, a mathematician that helped develop this technique). Function currying (as it's normally known), is the act of calling a function with less arguments than it needs and that function, instead of running with unpredicted results, returning a new function with the given arguments pre-set.

That was a mouthful, let's look at a very simple example that will clear things up:

```
//simple function
function add(x, y) { return x+y; }

//now we curry it
var curriedAdd  = curry(add);
var add100 = curriedAdd(100);

//now we simply...
console.log(add100(10)); //prints 110
```

Now, going back to the *partition* example from before, the function accepts two parameters, but I used it only with one; I passed in the property I want to group by, but not the list, so I *curried* the function and it, in turn, returned a new function that only requires the list of items to partition. This, of course, doesn't happen automatically in JavaScript; in order to achieve this, a hidden step is implied here, which consists of calling a currying function like I did with the add100 example.

But function currying, used properly, can be a great tool to help you get a clearer syntax, more declarative than imperative.

Let's look at a classic: Out of a list of user objects, get a list of user names; there are far too many ways to do that, but let's try to keep it functional, ok?

```
var users = [ {id: 1, name: 'Richard Reed' } , { id: 2, name: 'John Stewart' } ];

users.map(function(u) {  return u.name; }); //returns ['Richard Reed', 'John Stewart']
```

The code works, but if you're striving for declarative over imperative, the function definition on that one-liner feels wrong. So what if you curry that function, like so:

```
var get = curry(function(prop, o) { return o[prop]; });
```

The preceding declaration is a bit tricky. Remember, get is not actually the function you want; instead, the one you want is the function *returned* by get when called with the list of items you want to extract the property from. This way, you can use it with the likes of map, reduce, compose, etc. In this particular case, I was using map, so let's see how that would look now:

```
users.map(get('name'));
```

That was a lot clearer than before, wasn't it? And you can even go one step further if you curry the map call, like so:

```
var map = curry(function(list, fn) { return list.map(fn); });
//now we can do something like:
var listOfNames = map(get('name'));
```

And the best part of it? This code is not referencing the list of users at all. That means the listOfNames variable is referencing a function that you can reuse anywhere and even compose with another if you wanted.

As you can see, function currying provides a level of flexibility higher than what you're used to with simple functions; combine it with composition and you have a killer combo. Look at the following code, simply beautiful:

```
/*
The order of execution is the inverse of the order of the parameters,
so you have to read it backward:
* sort by id
* then get the name of the items, and join those names with a comma
*/
compose(
    compose(join(', '), map(get('name'))),
    sortBy(get('id'))
    );
```

Simple, clean, and the code almost reads like the comments—forget imperative programming!

Before I leave this subject alone, let's demistify the *curry* function, shall we? Here is a simple implementation that works for the previous examples:

```
function curry() {
    //We transform the arguments object into an array...
    var arrArguments = [].slice.call(arguments);
    var fn = arrArguments.splice(0, 1)[0];
    var headArgs = arrArguments;
    return function() { //the curried function
        var newArgs = headArgs.concat([].slice.call(arguments));
        return fn.apply(fn, newArgs);
    };
}

//Example usage

function sum(a, b) {
    return a + b;
}

var sum10 = curry(sum, 10);

console.log(sum10(1));
```

Since the function is meant to curry a function with as many parameters as you want, the list of parameters received is left blank, and it works directly with the *arguments* object, which contains all arguments received by the function. It takes the first one out of the list, since that's the function you're trying to curry; the rest are the arguments you're pre-setting.

It also returns an anonymous function, which will be the one calling your actual function, with the right list of arguments. As you can see, it is a very powerful function, with a very simple implementation.

The Tools of the Functional Programmer

So, what can you do with composition, pure functions, and currying? I'll tell you what you can do, you can create the three main functions any good functional programmer must know and love (yes, you'll either love them or hate them, because you'll be using them even without knowing).

Those functions are map, filterm and reduce. Let's get to know them a little better, although you might've used them already, since they're all part of the Array object. I'll show you how they work and what you can do with them.

Map

Let's start with the easiest of them. The map function is meant to apply a function to every element of your list, and with the results from that execution, it creates a new list.

I'll start with a basic example. Say you have a list of integers and you want to calculate the square root of each number, simple with map:

```
var numbers = [1, 2, 3, 4, 5, 6];
var results = numbers.map(function(i) { return Math.sqrt(i); } );
console.log(results);
/* Resulting on
[ 1,

  1.4142135623730951,

  1.7320508075688772,

  2,

  2.23606797749979,

  2.449489742783178 ]

*/
```

So, that was easy. There is even a simplification that can be applied to that, the method *Math.sqrt* receives one parameter and returns a value, kind of the same signature your anonymous function has, so you can directly write:

```
var numbers = [1, 2, 3, 4, 5, 6];
var results = numbers.map(Math.sqrt);
console.log(results);
```

The result is the same in both cases, but the second version is easier to understand, more declarative if you will.

CHAPTER 3 ■ FUNCTIONAL REACTIVE PROGRAMMING

There is a catch here, the applied function must be synchronous, it's not like you can do something like this:

```
var filenames = ['file1.txt', 'file2.txt' ];
var content = filenames.map(fs.readFile);
```

That won't work, because the readFile method is not returning the actual content, so you'll end up with an array full of undefined items if you try to run the preceding code, because again, the method I'm using doesn't return the content; in fact, it returns nothing at all. Fear not though, there is a way to do an asynchronous map and then use the resulting array, it's just a bit different.

Like with everything in the world of programming, there is not just one way to do this right, particularly. I'll show you two variants of this asynchronous map, one using ECMAScript 6 Promises (because, why not?) and another one using classic callback functions. You can pick the one you like the most and use that one.

```
//Map using ECMAScript 6 Promises
function promiseMap (list, fn) {

    var promises = list.map(function(i) {
        var p = new Promise(function(resolve, reject) {
            fn(i, function(err, result) {
                if(err) return reject(err);
                resolve(result);
            })
        });
        return p;
    });

    return Promise.all(promises);
}
```

The preceeding code is doing two simple things: First, it creates a list of promises and then it returns the promised returned by *Promise.all*, which will be resolved when all the promises you pass as parameter get resolved. And the "magic" happens inside the promises generated by for map loop, they execute the asynchronous function (*fn*), and depending on the results from that function, that promise either gets resolved or rejected, which, in turn, will impact the result of the general promise.

■ **Caution**   The preceding code clearly assumes that you already know what a Promise is and how you're supposed to use it. If you haven't, I encourage you to please go read up on the subject (https://developer. mozilla.org/en-US/docs/Web/JavaScript/Reference/Global_Objects/Promise).

And here is how you would use the new promise-based promiseMap function in your code:

```
//Sample code using promise based map function
var filenames = ['file1.txt', 'file2.txt'];
promiseMap(filenames, fs.readFile)
    .then(function(content) {
        console.log("------- Content of the files ---------");
        content.forEach(function(c) {
            console.log(c.toString());
```

```
        });
    })
    .catch(function(err) {
        console.error("There was an error reading your files: ", err);
    });
```

The sample code takes a list of strings (filenames) and applies the fs.readFile method to each one of them, basically reading each file and pouring its content into a new list. Once all items on the list have been processed, and all files have been successfully read, the final callback is called, and it will receive an array with all the results from the main function execution (fs.readFile).

Another way of dealing with asynchronous functions on a map call is using callbacks, and for that, you can go with a custom implementation like the one I'm about to show you or just rely on a third-party library, like Async.js(https://github.com/caolan/async).

```
//Map using regular callbacks
function callbackMap (list, fn, done) {

    var results = [];
    var counter = 0;

    list.forEach(function(i) {
        fn(i, function(err, result) {
            if(err) return done(err);
            results.push(result);
            counter++;
            if( counter == list.length ) {
                done(null, results);
            }
        });
    });
}
```

This code is a bit more straightforward than the promise-based one; simply iterate over all items, apply the async function, and keep track of how many callbacks are called. Once you reach the right number (equal to the number of items on the list), then you can call the done function and send the list of results.

Here's how you would go about using this function:

```
//Sample code using promise based map function
var filenames = ['file1.txt', 'file2.txt'];
callbackMap(filenames, fs.readFile, function(err, content) {
    if(err) {
        console.error("There was an error reading your files: ", err);
    } else {
        console.log("------- Content of the files ---------");
        content.forEach(function(c) {
            console.log(c.toString());
        });
    }
});
```

Now instead of setting up two callback functions using then and catch, you can set one anonymous function and receive both the error and the results, a classic callback pattern.

Filter

The `filter` function is another of the easy yet powerful tools of your functional arsenal. The idea behind it is simple: You iterate over a list of items, apply a boolean function to each item, and, if that function returns a TRUE value, add it to the returning list; otherwise, you ignore it, thus filtering the initial list.

Let's look at an example to fully understand the idea behind this function, which, again, is already part of the Array object in Node.js:

```
var list = [-4, -3, -2, 0, 2, 3, 4 ];
var positives = list.filter(function(nmbr) {  return nmbr > 0; });
console.log(positives); //this will of course print "[2, 3, 4]"
```

The basic idea here is that the filtering function needs to return a value and that value will be taken to either be thruthy (can be cast to boolean true) or falsy (can be cast to boolean false).

Dealing with asynchronous functions to perform the filtering is very similar to what you saw with map, so it is left to you as an exercise to implement that function.

An interesting usage you can give to `filter` using currying is the definition of reusable filters, you just need to make sure that unlike in the example from before, the first attribute to be received is the actual function to filter by:

```
/*
Custom implementation of a simple filter function
*/
function filter(filterFN, list) {
    var results [];
    list.forEach(function(item) {
        if(filterFN(item)) {
            results.push(item);
        }
    });
    return results;
}

var onlyEvenNumbers = curry(filter, function(nmbr) { return nmbr % 2 == 0; });
var list1 = [1,2,3,4,5,6,7,8,9,0];
var list2 = [-1, -4, -6, 23, 10];
var list3 = ['string', 'word', 4, 2, Date()];
 // now we can do
console.log(onlyEvenNumbers (list1)); //[ 2, 4, 6, 8, 0 ]
console.log(onlyEvenNumbers (list2)); //[ -4, -6, 10 ]
console.log(onlyEvenNumbers (list3)); //[ 4, 2 ]
```

Re-usability, again, yay! Such a powerful combo, *filter + curry*.

Reduce

And last but not least, reduce. This is definitely the most complex of the three, because its logic is not that straightforward, although, as you're about to see, it just requires you to pay a bit more attention to the explanation, that's all.

This function applies an operation to a cumulative value that starts at a custom value and each item on the list; the result of that operation is used in conjunction with the next, and so on, until the entire list is reduced to a single value.

That was a bit more complicated than I expected, so let's explain it with code, that and the definition should be more than enough to get you going:

```
var numbers = [1, 2, 3, 4, 5, 6, 7, 8, 9];
var sum = numbers.reduce(function add(x, y) { return x + y; }, 0);  //returns 45
```

Simple enough, let's go down over the above code's execution step by step:

```
result = add(0, 1) //this returns 1 obviously
result = add(result, 2); //this returns 3
result = add(result, 3); //this returns 6
result = add(result, 4); //this returns 10
result = add(result, 5); //this returns 15
result = add(result, 6); //this returns 21
result = add(result, 7); //this returns 28
result = add(result, 8); //this returns 36
result = add(result, 9); //this returns 45, and it's done!
```

Notice how you started with a 0, that's the second parameter you passed to the reduce method, that would be the initial value. But adding all numbers of a list is just a simple example; you'll probably find yourself doing other, more complex tasks, and reduce can help there too!

```
var words = [ 'Hello', ' ', 'world', '!' ];
var str = words.reduce(function(currentStr, word) {
    return currentStr += word;
}), '');
```

The preceeding code shows another classic example of the usage of the reduce method. Coincidently, I'm using the same operator (+), although instead of adding up numbers, I'm concatenating strings. Yes, there is a much easier way of doing the above with the join method, but of course, this is meant to provide an example of what can be done.

Finally, let's look at another example, a flatten function; it will receive a list of lists, and merge them all into a single, single levcer listo.

```
var listOfLists = [ [1, 2, 3], [ 4, 5 ] , [6, 7, 8] ];
var flattened = listOfLists.reduce(function(newList, item) {
        return newList.concat(item);
        }, []);
```

Putting It All Together

Just for the fun of it, let's end this subject with an example that uses most of the tools I've been mentioning for FP. It might help to give you a better idea on how they interact with each other.

Here's what you'll do: Read the content of a text file, get the ASCII code of every standard character, and finally, add up the numbers to get sum of all ASCII codes. Why are you doing this? Have you ever heard the rumor that the string 'Bill Gates III' turned to ASCII and then added up would return 666? Well, it's a pretty old rumor, so don't worry if you haven't heard it. What you'll do is use functional programming to either prove or debunk that rumor!

And because this is the chapter for it, I'll also throw in some reactive programming: Instead of having the filename hard-coded into some variable, I'll get the input from the user and use that string as the file name, add it to one of our Observable Streams, and set up a chain of functions that will

- Read the file using the input as file name.

- Split the resulting string into a character array.

- Filter out the unwanted characters.

- Map each character to it's ASCII code.

- Add them up.

- Print the resulting number out to console.

And here is the code:

```
var fs = require("fs");
var functionalUtils = require("./func_utils");
var ObservableStream = require("./ostream");

/*
Utility functions
*/
var filterUnwantedCharacters filter_unwanted_characters   =
functionalUtils.curry(functionalUtils.filter, function(c) {
    return /[a-zA-Z0-9 ]/.test(c);
});
var mapToInt = functionalUtils.curry(functionalUtils.map, function(c) {   return
c.charCodeAt(0); } );
var addUp = functionalUtils.curry(functionalUtils.reduce, function(x, y) { return x + y; });
var split = function(str) { return str.toString().split(""); };

//streams setup
var dataStream = new ObservableStream();

dataStream.data
    .then(fs.readFile)
    .then(split)
    .then(filterUnwantedCharactersfilter_unwanted_characters   )
    .then(mapToInt)
    .then(addUp)
    .then(console.log)
    .catch(function(error) { //Error handling!
        console.log("There was an error: ", error);
    })

var filenameStream = new ObservableStream();

var filename = "";
filenameStream.data
    .then(function(chr) {
        if(chr.charCodeAt(0) != 13) { //if we're not inputing an enter
            filename += chr;
```

```
        } else {
            dataStream.add(filename);
            filename = "";
        }
    });

var stdin = process.stdin;
stdin.setRawMode(true);
stdin.resume();
stdin.on('data', function(input) {
    var character = input.toString();
    console.log(character);
    if(character.charCodeAt(0) === 27) process.exit(0); //exit with ESC
    filenameStream.add(character);
});
```

You'll notice there are two libraries that I'm requiring that are actually custom (func_utils and ostream), but the code is not there, I'll show you their code further down the book; right now, it's enough to know that we're using the functions I've already discussed. As for the *ObservableStream* object, just don't worry too much about it; I'll cover it in detail shortly.

■ **Note**   By the way, if you tried the code that comes with the book and used a file with the content "Bill Gates III," you've probably seen that the rumor was terribly wrong. So, bummer, but at least you got to debunk it AND have some fun at the same time!

The code is actually pretty straightforward, but, like always, there are a couple of interesting bits, so let's go over them.

Two Streams Instead of One

I'm using two streams, one to gather the filename from the user's input. There is only one function on the chain of events for this one. I could probably handle it differently, using some form of custom concat function, but for simplicity reasons, this version of it will do.

Once this custom function detects we've hit the ENTER key, it'll add the current string to our other stream, the one that takes care of processing everything and returning the magic number.

For the second stream, I've setup a slightly longer chain of events meant to process the file's content step by step and print out the final result. They do everything I mentioned before, so there is nothing new to add here.

Curry the Hell Out of the Functions

To make things easier to read and, just as important, compatible with the Observable Streams chain of events, I curried all the main functions. That is, filtering, reducing, and mapping, they all got curried into a simplified and customized version. There was no need to curry the split function, since it only required one parameter.

Readability ++

The logic behind the code is very simple, I simply wanted to read a file, transform it's content into ASCII code and find out the resulting number. But I dare you to write it using traditional, imperative logic. Leave aside all the tools I've been talking about and write it without them. The abstraction level will go down, and you'll find yourself trying to solve other problems that I didn't even have to touch.

So that's declarative programming for you, and we should definitely talk about it some more, so let's discuss.

Declarative Programming

An immediate side effect from using a declarative approach on your code is (as I've said it countless times) the opportunity to write declarative statements in your programs instead of the usual imperative ones.

Put simply, using the tools you saw above, you can write code that *describes* what you want to accomplish, instead of what you normally learn to do, which is tell the compiler/interpreter how to do what you think is best, to accomplish the results you want.

Although there are some languages that are purely declarative, like SQL, XSL, and Prolog, thanks to JavaScript's ability to allow you to write functional code, you can count JS as a partially descriptive programming language. All that's required is the developer's willingness to do so.

Make no mistake, imperative programming is just as valid a way of writing code as it is declarative programming, and it makes total sense that it has been the first thing you're taught when starting out; after all, with the first computers, with their vacuum tubes and a very basic instruction set, the developers were forced to write their programs in a step-by-step manner, telling them exactly how to solve everything.

Let's now look at an example of how much your code's readability can change going from a purely (or maybe mostly) imperative implementation into a more declarative one.

```
getRemoteData("www.remoteurl.com", function(err, data) {
    if(err) {
        return handleError(err);
    }

    parseData(data, function(err, items) {
        if(err) {
            return handleError(err);
        }
        var names = [];
        for(var i = 0; i < items.length; i++) {
            if(items[i].age > 18) {
                names.push(items[i].name);
            }
        }
        console.log(names.join(", "));
    });
});
```

The preceding code is a perfect example of imperative code. You are

- Manually checking for errors whenever you're supposed to get them.

- Creating a local variable for the sole purpose of iterating over each element of an array.

- Creating an extra array simply to temporarily store the extracted names of the objects.

The code works, and the problem is not that it is inefficient or that it might have bugs. No, the main issue here is

- You have to mentally parse the code. Granted it is not that complex of an algorithm, but the cognitive load is there, you have to do it if you want to understand what the code is trying to do.

- Extending that code requires, again, that you read it and understand the effects of your changes over the entire algorithm.

Let's now think in a declarative way. Basically you want to think on *what* needs to be done, instead of jumping into the *how*. You want to

- Get the data from the remote url.

- Parse the results.

- Get the names of the objects that are over 18 years old.

- Print the list of comma-separated names.

Now that's the list of steps you want your app to do, but there is nothing in there that tells you *how* it is meant to do it. And that's fine, you don't need to, because you already have the tools that will handle the "low level" tasks of iterating over items, or getting the property of an object, or chaining the steps so that you don't need to worry about callbacks, and the list can go on.

So let's take a quick look at what your algorithm would look like if you were to write it declaratively:

```
getRemoteData("ww.remoteurl.com")
        .then(parseData)          //gets a response object and returns a list of objects
        .then(filter(over18))
        .then(map(get('name')))   //gets the names of each object
        .then(join(", "))         //gets a list of strings and returns a string
        .then(console.log)        //finally print out the string
        .catch(handleError);      //one single line for the error handler
```

The code has a very promise-like structure, so reading it is very easy. The steps shown on the chain of calls are pretty much the same steps we described earlier, so you can see how declarative out code is.

I'm using some functional tools you've already seen, like map and get, and some new ones, like join (another curried function that reproduces the join method of the String objects) or the ability to pipe the results of one function into the parameters of another one.

Adding a step into the above flow is considerably easier than doing it with the imperative alternative, since you don't have to deal with any code. Just make sure the input and output of your function corresponds to the place in the chain where you want to add it.

What Every FRP Language Must Have

Now that you've got the basics of what FP is, and you had a quick overview of declarative programming, you have the tools you'll need to start talking about FRP.

Although JavaScript is not a purely functional reactive language, and there are others that are, like Haskell or Elm (http://elm-lang.org), I'll go over the main thing any FRP languages must have and then I'll compare that to JavaScript, and you'll see how you can implement such a feature in your favorite language.

Observable Streams

The main characteristic of a functional reactive language should be the ability to have native observable streams of events. During Chapters 1 and 2, I covered how important these streams are. They're basically the stepping stone to the *Reactive* part of the language.

These are the constructs that, when updated, your code will react to, so they're pretty important, mind you! So, what are they, exactly? What are they supposed to look like? There are many ways to explain them, but the easiest way to think of them is like a composition of the Observer Pattern and the Iterator Pattern.

On one side, the Observer Pattern dictates:

- There are two types of objects related to the pattern, the Subject, which is the observed object, and the Observers, which are, well, the objects that will react to updates on the subject.

- The subject maintains the list of its observers.

- When the subject's state changes, all observers are notified by it. Normally executing a pre-established method (usually called *notify*)

Let's now take a look at Figure 3-1 for a visual explanation of what the Observer Pattern looks like.

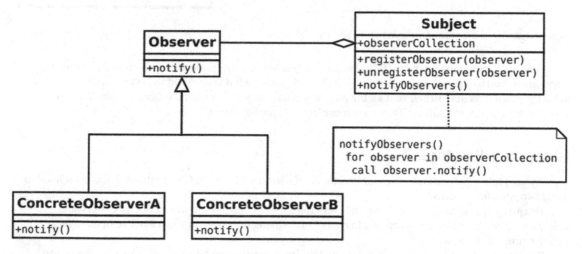

Figure 3-1. *UML diagram for the Observer Pattern (public domain image from Wikipedia page on Observer Pattern)*

Figure 3-1 shows a classic implementation of this pattern, including the mentioned *notify* method and the logic for notifying the observers. Now, this pattern is great but it lacks one minor detail: While the producer is sending events one after another to all consumers, there is no well-defined way to tell them that there are no more events. I'll get back to this later.

Now, with the Iterator Pattern, you have a much simpler pattern than with the Observer Pattern. Here, you're just trying to decouple the algorithm required to traverse a collection, from the actual implemenation of the collection. The main advantage being that you can re-use the traversing algorithm over different types of collections. Figure 3-2 provides a visual explanation for this pattern.

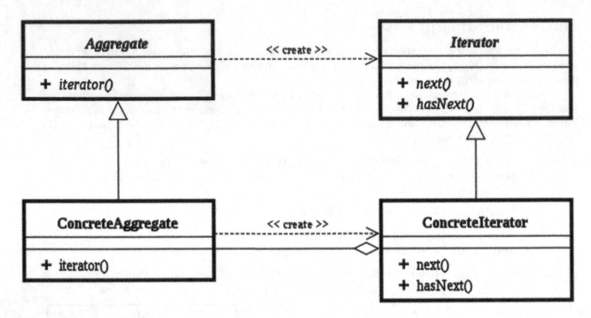

Figure 3-2. *UML diagram for the Iterator Pattern*

Figure 3-2 shows the textbook UML diagram for this pattern. The collection (which is extending the Aggregate class) can create an iterator, and it will provide the methods required to get an item from it and to ask if there is a next item to get. That's a big plus over what you just saw with the Observer Pattern, because now you have a way of knowing if there are more items in the list or not.

Observer + Iterator = ?

So, why am I talking about Observer and Iterator all of a sudden? How are Observable collections related to these two specific patterns?

You just saw that the Observer Pattern is very reminiscent of what you want from an Observable collection, since the producer is actually in charge of notifying the observers, just like I've been saying reactive programming works.

But you also saw how that model is not enough if you also want to be aware of the end of the stream of updates. How can you tell when the observed object is done sending updates?

And here is where the iterator pattern comes into play. With it, you can tell when the end of the stream comes and you even have a very clean (and more importantly *standard*) way of snatching updates from the stream.

In other words, an *Observable stream* is a dynamically updated collection with a standard interface to iterate over it.

So let's see what a native observable stream looks like on a Functional Reactive language like Elm:

```
import Graphics.Element exposing (..)
import Mouse

main : Signal Element
main =
  Signal.map show Mouse.position
```

The syntax of Elm might be unfamiliar to you but the idea of what the code is trying to accomplish should be fairly obvious given the declarative nature of the code and the incredibly low number of code lines on the snippet.

The code (taken from one of Elm's website examples http://elm-lang.org/examples/mouse-position) is printing onscreen the coordinates for the mouse pointer position and updating it every time you move the mouse. The Mouse.position property is actually an observable stream, which is used as input to the Signal.map method, which is applying the show function to each new value of the stream. Like I said, super easy!

What would your JavaScript code look like, if you wanted to do the same, using the declarative syntax I've been showing you so far? Something along these lines:

```
Mouse.getPosition()
      .then(map(show));
```

Then how would you go about implementing an Observable Stream on JavaScript (more specifically using Node.js)? Here is a basic approach at that problem:

```
var EE = require("events");
var util = require("util");

function ObservableStream() {
    this.values = [];
    this.error_fn = null;
    EE.call(this);
}

util.inherits(ObservableStream, EE);

ObservableStream.prototype.add = function(value) {
    this.values.push(value);
    this.emit('data', value);
};

ObservableStream.prototype.getValues = function(){
    var self = this;
    var stream = new Streamable();

    self.on('data', function(v) {
        stream.emit('trigger', v)
    })

    return stream;
};
```

The preceding code is the main class the developer should focus on, the public one if you will, and it provides the entrance point to the actual heart of the library, which is the Streamable class (see next). The way this code works is simply by emitting a data event every time a new item is added to the internal collection (which is why I'm using the EventEmitter module). As you can see on the getValues method, the Streamable object is listening to this event, and every time the event is triggered, the streamable itself fires a new trigger event, to start the chain of transformations.

```javascript
function Streamable(triggerCode) {
    this.events = []
    this.idx = 0;
}

Streamable.prototype.start = function(val) {
    this.idx = 0;
    this.next(val);
};

Streamable.prototype.next = function(val, result) {
    if(this.idx >= this.events.length) return false;
    var currentFn = this.events[this.idx]

    this.idx++;
    currentFn(val);
};

Streamable.prototype.catch = function(errfn) {
    this.error_fn = errfn;
};

Streamable.prototype.then = function(fn) {
    var self = this;
    var newFn = null;
    if(!fn.__type) { //if it's not one of our helper functions...
        if(fn.length > 1) { // checking the number of arguments a function receives. If it's
        higher than 1, we're assuming the second parameter is the done callback
            newFn = function(val) {
                fn(val, function(err, result) {
                    if(err) return self.error_fn(err);
                    self.next(result);
                });
            };
        } else {
            newFn = function(val) {
                    self.next(fn(val));
                };
        }
    } else { //if it is...
        if(fn.__type === 'map') {
            newFn = function(val) {
                    self.next(fn(val))
                };
        }
    }
    if(newFn)
        this.events.push(newFn);
    return this; // we return the object, so we
};
```

The Streamable class provides the famous then method, and every function that is passed to it is wrapped into another function (that handles the call to the next function on the chain of events) and added to a list. Once the trigger event is fired, the class will iterate over that list and call one function after another.

```
//Helper map function. This is how a curried function looks:
function map(fn) {
    var curried = function(val) {
        return fn(val);
    }
    curried.__type = 'map'; //custom parameter so our then function knows how to handle us
    return curried;
}
```

■ **Note** You probably noticed that the error handling is pretty basic; that is, of course, for simplicity reasons. The final code will have all the error handling it needs.

One extra enhancement that can be made to this code, just to make it a bit more declarative, would be to replace the *getValues* method with a property defined with a setter. So we just remove the method altogether, and inside the constructor, we add the following code:

```
function ObservableStream() {
    this.values = [];
    this.error_fn = null;
    EE.call(this);
    Object.defineProperty(this, 'data', {
        get: function() { //getValues' old code
            var self = this;
            var stream = new Streamable();

            self.on('data', function(v) {
                stream.start(v)
            })
            return stream;
        }
    });
}
```

Now the getValues method is no longer required, you can simply use the *data* property.

And here is an example that uses the above code to transform and work with an ObservableStream:

```
//We instantiate the Observable Stream and set up the chain of transformations we'll apply to it.
var fs = require("fs");

var dataStream = new ObservableStream();
```

```
dataStream.data
    .then(map(function(x) {
        return 'filename_' + x + '.txt';
    }))
    .then(fs.readFile)
    .then(map(function(x) {
        return '' + x;
    }))
    .then(console.log);

//The events for our stream will be generated by us when we press a key on our keyboard.
var stdin = process.stdin;
stdin.setRawMode(true);
stdin.resume();
stdin.on('data', function(input) {
    var str = input.toString();
    dataStream.add(str)
    if(str == 'x') { //exit condition so we're not listening for keystrokes until the end of time
        process.exit();
    }
});
```

There are two main sections in the preceding code. The first one sets everything up for the Observable Stream; it instantiates it and it also sets up the chain of transformations. The second half of the code represents an external source of data.

Let's first cover the latter, since it's where everything starts, from the dataflow perspective anyway. This block of code basically allows you to capture the event fired every time the user presses a key on the keyboard. With that event, you just cast the object received to String and add it to your custom collection. The extra if statement is just there to make sure you can stop listening and close the program whenever you want.

This code could be anything, the important thing here is that you're adding values to your observable collection when they come. Where are they coming from? That's irrelevant.

Now, the first block of the code from before is where you set up the chain of functions that will handle the data coming from the stream. They're pretty straightforward, which corresponds to what I mentioned earlier in this chapter: Descriptive code is much easier to read and mentally parse.

The steps are very simple. For every key pressed:

1. Turn that character into a filename with the map function.

2. Then pass that into the fs.readFile method, so it will read the file with that name.

3. There is an extra step here, where you cast the buffer returned into an actual String.

4. And finally, the output from step 3 (the content of the file read) is passed to this last step, which basically prints it out with *console.log*.

Yes, the logic is pretty simple, but the beauty of it is that you're focusing on that, not on how to read the file, handle errors, and all that low level jazz.

Summary

This was a big chapter, I covered a lot in it, and you also got to have some fun while reading it—at least I hope you did!

So to recap, the chapter covered:

- Major points about functional programming in JavaScript, you saw what it meant for a piece of code to be considered functional, you went over the main principles, and you even covered some of the must-know tools any functional programmer should master.

- You also covered, again, the benefits of declarative programming over the good-old imperative approach.

- And then you moved into Observable Streams, which are the cornerstone of functional reactive programming library. I showed you how they're supposed to work, and I even went over the implementation of one.

For the next chapter, I will cover how RP is meant to help on the back-end, since RP is normally used for front-end development.

■ ■ ■

CHAPTER 4

Reactive Programming on the Back-end

Now that you know what you're dealing with, it is finally time to start getting your hands dirty. In this chapter, I'm going to analyze how you can take the advantages that functional reactive programming (FRP) provides and apply them to the back-end.

To do that, I will go over a set of sample common use cases for back-end programmers, look at a regular implementation, and then take the FRP road and re-implement the same use case.

Since I don't have a FRP module developed by myself nor picked from the list of available ones, I will assume I have a custom one already developed. This will help me in two fronts:

- It will provide the required support the code needs.

- It will help define the API for the soon-to-be-developed FRP module. Right now I'll assume I have it, and that every function/method needed is already available.

By the end of this chapter, you'll have all the justification you need to start going Reactive on your back-end code. And to do that, I'll go over two very common use cases:

- Simple API with CRUD endpoints: I'll create a simple API that provides a single endpoint with all the CRUD (Create, Retrieve, Update and Delete) functionalities you need.

- Login: An endpoint for retrieving authentication tokens will be added to the previously developed API.

So without further ado, let's get to it.

API with CRUD Endpoints

This is probably one of the most common use cases out there for any back-end developer. Most likely, you must have encountered at least one or two of these features in the past, but I'll look at the full set of CRUD functions.

Obviously, there are too many ways to implement this, and each one is just as valid as the next, so for the purpose of this example, let's define some constraints.

© Fernando Doglio 2016

F. Doglio, *Reactive Programming with Node.js*, DOI 10.1007/978-1-4842-2152-5_4

The Models

The API will deal with two models, that way it'll also include some logic dealing with the relationship of both of them. In particular, the models will be User and Address. Each user will have a set of addresses and they will have the following structure:

- **User**
  - first_name: String
  - last_name: String
  - birth_date: Date
  - addresses: [Address]
- Address
  - street_name: String
  - house_number: Number
  - phone_number: String

■ **Tip** Attributes like an Id, the creation date, or any other mandatory basic one are left out of the list and assumed added to the models by the framework being used.

The API

Table 4-1 is the list of endpoints that the API will provide with the code. They're mainly the bare minimum needed to provide a RESTful interface to deal with the resources represented by the models.

Table 4-1. *List of Endpoints for the API Being Developed*

HTTP Method	URL	Description
GET	/users/	Returns the list of users
GET	/users/:id	Returns the information for one specific user (given by the id parameter on the url)
POST	/users	Creates a new user on the database
POST	/users/:id/addresses	Adds an address to the list of addresses of a given user
PUT	/users/:id	Updates the information of one particular user (note that this does not update the information of an address model)
DELETE	/users/:id	Removes the user (and its associated addresses) from the database

The Standard Implementation

In order to implement the aforementioned specs, I'll use a set of standard modules, in particular, Express. JS(available at `http://expressjs.com/`) will be the web framework of choice (because let's face it, it is the de facto standard when it comes to web frameworks for Node.js). I'll also be using Mongoose (http://mongoosejs.com/) as an ORM for the storage layer, which will be done over MongoDB (this is simply because the lack of schema will simplify the development of this use case).

I'll organize the code into three files: `models-crud-api.js` will have the definition of both schemas and it will export a dictionary of all the defined schemas; `routes-crud-api.js` will have the definition for all enpdoints of the API, and it will export the router object used to define them; and finally `main-crud-api.js`, which will simply contain the main code for the API.

Let's take a quick look at how that code would look like:

`routes-crud-api.js`

```
var router = require("express").Router(),
    models = require("./models-crud-api");

router.get('/', function(req, res, next) {
    models.users.find({})
        .populate('addresses')
            .then(res.json.bind(res))//we make sure the 'this' is correct when the function
            is called
        .catch(next);
});

router.get('/:id', function(req, res, next) {
    models.users.findById(req.params.id)
        .populate("addresses")
        .then(function(usr) {
            if(!usr) {
                return res.status(404).json({
                    error: true,
                    msg: 'User not found'
                });
            }
            return res.json(usr);
        })
        .catch(next);
});

router.post('/', function(req, res, next) {

    models.users.create(req.body)
        .then(function(usr) {
            res.json(usr);
        })
        .catch(next);
});
```

```
router.post('/:id/addresses', function(req, res, next){

    var addressPromise = models.addresses.create(req.body);
    var userPromise = addressPromise.then(function(address) {
      return models.users.findById(req.params.id)
    });

    Promise.all([addressPromise, userPromise], function([address, user]) {
      user.addresses.push(address._id);
      return user.save();
    }).then(function(user) {
      return res.json(user);
    }).catch(next);
});

router.put('/:id', function(req, res, next) {
    models.users
        .findByIdAndUpdate(req.params.id, req.body, {new: true}) //{new: true} makes sure
            the updated document  is returned
        .then(function(usr) {
            res.json(usr);
        })
        .catch(next);
});

router.delete('/:id', function(req, res, next) {
    models.users
        .findByIdAndRemove(req.params.id)
        .then(function() {
            res.sendStatus(200);
        })
        .catch(next);
});

module.exports = router;
```

From the above code, you can see that the main logic for the endpoints is not that complicated; you can pretty much map each one to a helper method provided by Mongoose, with the clear exception of /:id/ addresses, which requires you to do a small amount of thinking in order to understand it (first creating the address and then updating the user with the reference, all of it using promises).

models-crud-api.js

```
var usersSchema = Schema({
    first_name: {
        type: String,
        required: true
    },
    last_name: {
        type: String,
        required: true
```

```
    },
    birth_date: Date,
    addresses: [
    {
        ref: 'Address',
        type: Schema.Types.ObjectId
    }]
});
```

■ **Tip**   Although normal JS code convention is camelCase, the fields used for the models are expressed using snake_case because that is the default standard for MongoDB.

```
var usersModel = mongoose.model('User', usersSchema);

module.exports = {
    users: usersModel,
    addresses: addressModel
};
```

Entities schemas and models definition and final models dictionary export; the rest is your run-of-the-mill code, and there is nothing relevant to mention about it.

main-crud-api.js

```
var express = require("express"),
    bodyParser = require("body-parser"),
    mongoose = require("mongoose"),
    userRouter = require("./routes-crud-api");

var app = express();

app.use(bodyParser.json());

app.use('/users', userRouter);

//Generic error handler
app.use(function(err, req, res, next) {
    console.error("--- Error encountered ---");
    console.error(err);
    res.status(500).json({
        msg: err,
        error: true
    });
});

mongoose.connect('mongodb://localhost/test-chapter4');
var db = mongoose.connection;
```

```
db.once('open', function() {
    console.log("Database connection established...");
    app.listen(3004, function() {
        console.log("Server started ...");
    });
});
```

The final or, actually, main file for this example and the two relevant bits to mention about it are listed here.

The generic error handler defined; this function will be called from the endpoint's code when the *catch* statement is executed. This is very easy to test: Simply try to create a user leaving out the last name, that will cause a validation error, which will trigger the *catch* clause, which, in turn, will call next with the error parameter, causing the error handler to be called.

The last few lines show how you can start the web server on port 3004, but only after the connection to the database has been established (that is what that open event means). This is a pretty standard and safe way of initializing your application, making sure all services are up, before starting the web server.

The Functional Reactive Implementation

This implementation should be different, but not in every way. I'm not trying to rewrite the web server, or the ORM into being fully reactive; instead, I'm just trying to implement the business logic using this paradigm.

In this particular example, this translates to rewriting the router-related code, since that's where its main logic lays. And in order to do that, I'll transform the endpoints into observable collections, where every new request is a new event added. With that in mind, I'll apply a set of transformations to that event that will render the results as you need it in every case.

The Router File

Let's first take a look at this file back on the previous implementation; that was where all the logic was written, but it was also where the route matching was done by Express. For this implementation, I'll remove the business logic from there and only leave route matching, and here is what that code looks like:

```
var collections = require("./collections-rfrp  "),
    router = require("express").Router(),
    _ = require("lodash");

var mapping = {
    '/': {
        'get': collections.listUsersCollection,
        'post': collections.newUsersCollection
    },
    '/:id': {
        'get': collections.getUserDataColection,
        'put': collections.updateUserCollection,
        'delete': collections.deleteUsersCollection
    },
    '/:id/addresses': {
        'post': collections.newAddressCollection
    }
};
```

This JSON is mapping every endpoint to a different observable collection, and the following code takes care of adding the request, the response, and the next function received upon every request to the corresponding collection.

```
//we set up the urls
_.each(mapping, function (actions, url) {
    _.each(actions, function(collection, method) {
        router[method](url, function() { //this is the code that every route will actually execute
            collection.add(arguments);  //we pass the arguments object because we want to
                have access to all three parameters in one
        });
    });
});

module.exports = router;
```

As I mentioned before, the code is very simple. This isn't really reactive or anything; instead, it just takes care of adding the new events to the corresponding collections.

The New Business Logic

As is evidenced from the above code, each endpoint's logic got moved into a separate ObservableStream object, this way you can transform the streams accordingly. Let's first compare each transformation code side by side with it's homologue on the original implementation.

Listing All Users

The regular code for this case is pretty simple. In this case, what you need is to do the following:

- Requests all users.
- Populate their addresses.
- Print the result as a JSON object.

Figure 4-1 shows you how you would go about designing the reactive version using a marbles diagram.

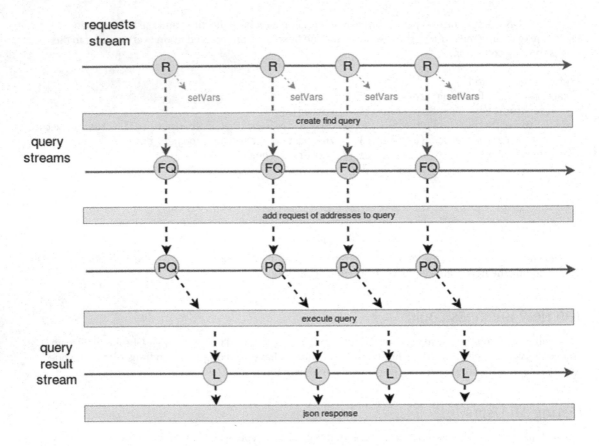

Figure 4-1. *Marble diagram for the reactive version of listing users*

It went from a stream of HTTP requests into a stream of query objects and ended up being a stream of query results (which are then printed out to the HTTP client in JSON format). Table 4-2 shows the implementation of the diagram in Figure 4-1.

Table 4-2. *Side-by-Side Comparison of the Code for Listing Users*

Reactive Code	Regular Implementation
```var list = new oStream(); list.data .setVars({'httpResponse': get(1), 'next': get(2)}) .then(find({})) .then(populate('addresses')) .then(execute) .done(toJSONResponse) .catch(callErrorHandler);```	```router.get('/', function(req, res, next) { models.users.find({}) .populate('addresses') .then(res.json.bind(res)) .catch(next); });```

It's true, our new version has more code than the old one, but that is sometimes an unfortunate side effect of a higher level of abstraction. It might be difficult to see the benefits of our approach with solely this example, so let's keep going.

■ **Note** You might have noticed that in the previous comparison the reactive code does not show the router-related part while the regular implementation does. This is because for the reactive version of the application, I have split the routing and the actual business logic, while on the regular version they were both the same.

The helper functions are described further ahead in this chapter, so don't worry if you don't understand how they work just yet. You will.

Creating a New User

Creating users is another of the simple ones, since it relies entirely on the ORM's methods. Still let's take a look at how you would structure your logic in Figure 4-2.

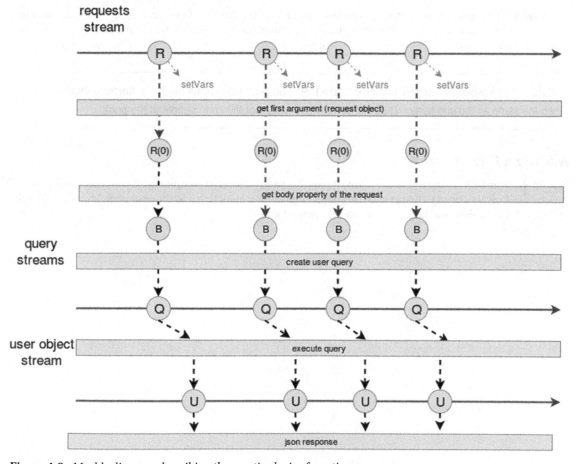

Figure 4-2. *Marble diagram describing the reactive logic of creating a new user*

Sadly, because you're dealing with a non-reactive web framework, you have to manually deal with the parameters of the request (which is what the first step of the process is). After that, you just get the body of the request, create and perform the save query, and, finally, return the JSON representation of the new user.

Now take a look at Table 4-3 for a view of the new code.

Table 4-3. *Side-by-Side Comparison of the Code Required to Create a New User*

Reactive Code	Regular Code
| ```
newUsers.data
    .setVars({'httpResponse': get(1),
    'next': get(2)})
    .then(get(0))
    .then(get('body'))
    .then(models.users.create.bind
    (models.users))
    .done(toJSONResponse)
    .catch(callErrorHandler);
``` | ```
router.post('/', function(req, res, next) {
    models.users.create(req.body)
        .then(function(usr) {
        res.json(usr);
        })
        .catch(next);
});
``` |

One thing to note about the code is that since you're passing the create method from Mongoose on the 4th then call, you need to correctly bind it to the model. Otherwise the function will be executed without a context and it will fail.

■ **Note**   I'll skip over the update a user, delete a user ,and get a user's data methods, because they're pretty much the same as the one earlier. They will be provided as part of the code bundle of the book.

Adding a New Address

The final method I'll review is this one, since it presents an extra level of complexity. If you remember from the code before, you need to first create the address entity, then associate it to the user somehow. Take a look at Figure 4-3 to understand how the reactive logic would look.

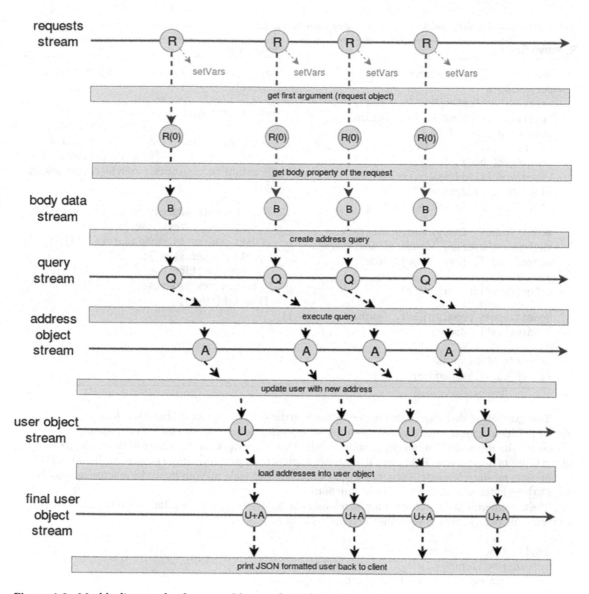

Figure 4-3. *Marble diagram for the new address endpoint's reactive version*

If you remember (go back a few pages if you don't), the original code combined two promises to achieve its goal. The preceding diagram shows a rather longer (steps-wise, I mean) solution, but a more direct one as well. If you look at it, the solution is pretty straightforward. Take a look at Table 4-4 for the code comparison.

Table 4-4. *Side-by-Side Comparison of the Code Required to Create a New Address for a User.*

Reactive Code	Regular Code
| ```
var newAddress = new oStream();
newAddress.data
    .setVars({'httpResponse': get(1),
    'userId': function(args) { return
    args[0].params.id}})
    .then(get(0))
    .then(get('body'))
    .then(models.addresses.create.
    bind(models.addresses))
    .then(function(address, done) {

    models.users.findByIdAndUpdate(this.
    customVars.userId, {$push: {'addresses':
    address.id}}, {new: true}, done);
    })
    .then(function(usr, done) {

    models.users.populate(usr, {path:
    'addresses'}, done);
    })
    .done(toJSONResponse)
    .catch(callErrorHandler );
``` | ```
router.post('/:id/addresses', function(req,
res, next){

    var addressPromise = models.addresses.
                         create(req.body);
    var userPromise = addressPromise.then
                      (function(address) {
      return models.users.findById(req.params.id)
    });

    Promise.all([addressPromise, userPromise],
      function([address, user]) {
      user.addresses.push(address._id);
      return user.save();
    }).then(function(user) {
      return res.json(user);
    }).catch(next);
});
``` |

This example is also showing more lines of code on the reactive approach, but if you look at the regular implementation, once the business logic's complexity increased, extra tools were required, either promises (with the added complexity of understanding how they work) or good old callback logic, with the added levels of indentation. Either way the reactive approach keeps things under control, with one level of indentation, maybe a few extra steps; but if you extrapolate and scale up your logic, the reactive approach starts to look better and better. The helper functions

The aforementioned reactive examples reference several helper functions that I haven't shown yet. I'll list their code here, simply to show they're mostly one-liners.

```
var find = function(where, done) {
    return function() {
        return models.users.find(where, done);
    }
};

var populate = function(what) {
    return function(query) {
        return query.populate(what);
    };
};

var execute = function(query, done) {
    return query.exec(done);
};
```

```
var findById = function(id) {
    return models.users.findById(id);
};

var findByIdAndUpdate = function(params, done) {
    return models.users.findByIdAndUpdate(params[0], params[1], {new: true} ,done);
};

var findByIdAndDelete = function(id, done) {
    return models.users.findByIdAndRemove(id, done);
};

var toJSONResponse = function(data) {
    return this.customVars.httpResponse.json(data);
};

var callErrorHandler = function(err) {
    return this.customVars.next(err);
};
```

The interesting bit to reference here is how some of these functions are pulling properties of their this object, although it is never declared anywhere. That is because the context of all functions passed to the then method, gets extended with the properties of the Stream to which it is being associated. This means that if a function has no context set, it'll be that of the Stream, which makes it easy to access properties such as customVars, which contains the extra variables declared by setVars.

In Conclusion

By looking at the previous code (or the complete bundled code that is available with this book), you can see that the premise of using an Observable Stream to handle HTTP incoming traffic is perfectly possible. Not only that, but it helps keep code complexity under check.

Things like middlewares are also possible. I'll look into that in the next example.

Log-in Service

The ability to log into your application is another of those features you've probably done in the past—several times in fact, if you've been doing application development for a while. I'll look into one particular example, which is authentication against a RESTful API using a JSON Web Token.

This way, you'll be able to extend the previous example, add the authentication endpoint, and, finally, protect some of the endpoints by setting up a middleware into the chain of transformations you have setup for every collection.

What Is a JSON Web Token?

In case you were wondering, let me do a quick re-cap of what a JSON Web Token (JWT) is and how it will help you achieve what you want.

A JWT (http://jwt.io) is an open standard (you can find its RFC at https://tools.ietf.org/html/rfc7519) that defines a way of safely transferring information between two sides. This is achieved by digitally signing the data transferred—in this case, the request sent from the client to the server. The data can be signed either with a secret phrase using an HMAC algorithm or using a private/public key pair using RSA.

Either way, it allows developers to authenticate their requests against a RESTful service, because it doesn't require them to maintain any state about the entity being authenticated. In order to corroborate the authenticity of the request, the signed token is decoded and verified using the contract previously stated between client and server. If the verification is successful, then the request is valid.

The token itself is calculated in three simple steps:

- A JSON header is set, which contains the type of token (which in this case is JWT) and the algorithm used to sign it, something like the following example. Then the data are encoded into base 64.

```
{
"alg": "HS256",
"typ": "JWT"
}
```

- The payload is created using information related to the request, normally this is information about the user (since that is the constant part in all requests). This JSON is then encoded using base 64.

```
{
    "name": "John Doe",
    "isAdmin": true
}
```

- Finally, the token is created by concatenating both base 64 strings from this example and signing that using the algorithm defined in the first step. The resulting token looks something like this:

eyJhbGciOiJIUzI1NiIsInR5cCI6IkpXVCJ9.
eyJuYW1lIjoiUFdEEIiwiaWFOIjoxNDYONDQxMTc4LCJleHAiOjEONjQ1Mjc1Nzh9.
oc194WsEKcRe29FuUKS9XdvKpX72ntONuN5FAUVicW4

And here is how you would use the JWT token to provide security to your API:

- The user makes an unauthenticated request to an endpoint sending his/her credentials, in order to authenticate against the system.

- The API checks the credentials, and if they're valid, then a JWT token is generated and returned to the user.

- The user then will use that token for any subsequent request to authenticate without having to re-send the credentials.

- If the system is able to verify the authenticity of the token, then the request is carried out, otherwise an error response is returned.

Figure 4-4 shows the flow between client and server when dealing with JWTs.

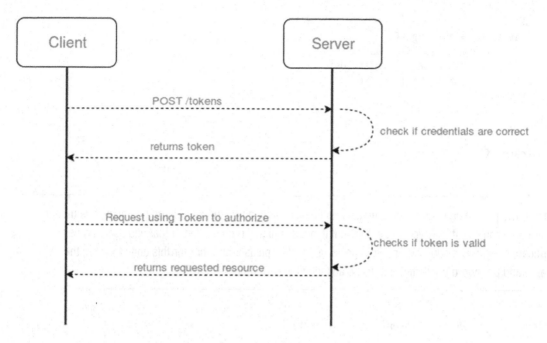

Figure 4-4. *Client-server interaction during the authentication process*

Back to the Code

Let's get back on track, shall we? Now that you understand how JWT-based authentication works, let's see how you can implement that using traditional programming on the back-end, using ExpressJS. To generate and verify your tokens, you'll use an NPM module called *jsonwebtoken* (available at https://www.npmjs.com/package/jsonwebtoken), which provides all the required functionality.

For this implementation, I'll extend the code from the previous example. All I need are two methods, one to handle the new token endpoint and one to handle the verification of the token on every request. I'll use a middleware for the second code, since it's the more reasonable approach.

```
var router = require("express").Router();
var jwt = require("jsonwebtoken");
var models = require("./models-crud-api  ");

var SECRET =  'this is a secret phrase';

//Handle the new endpoint
router.post('/tokens', function(req, res, next) {
    models.users.findOne({
        username: req.body.username,
        password: req.body.password
    })
    .then(function(usr) {
        if(!usr) {
            return next({error: true, msg: 'User not valid  '});
```

```
        }
        var token = jwt.sign({
                name: usr.first_name,
                birth_date: usr.birth_date
                }, SECRET , {"expiresIn": "1 day "});
        res.json({
            token: token
        });
    })
    .catch(next);
});
```

■ **Note**   The preceding code is handling user authentication in a very unsecure and poor way; it is meant to provide an example of how you could go about it, but it is highly recommended that you use a proper authentication technique (like SALTing your passwords). Also, please note that for this code to work, the username and password properties should be added to the user model.

```
function check_token checkToken(req, res, next) {

    var token = req.query.token || req.headers.token;

    //we make sure the url required for requesting a token is not protected
    if(req.url.indexOf("/tokens") !== -1) return next();

    if(!token) {
        return next('No token provided');
    }

    jwt.verify(token, SECRET, function(err, decoded) {
        if(err) {
            return next(err);
        }
        next();
    });
}

module.exports = {
    router: router,
    checkToken: checkToken
};
```

On the preceding code, the endpoint function takes care of a simple validation of the user's credentials; if they're valid, then it'll sign the token to be returned. Then the checkToken middleware takes care of securing the endpoints, with the exception of /tokens since you can't really send a token before actually getting it from the system, can you?

The Reactive Approach

For the reactive version of this code, I'll create the logic for the new endpoint, which, of course, will be a set of transformations over the stream, and I'll also show you how to implement the token check as part of the transformations instead of using the middleware (which, in this case, because I'm keeping the main code intact, I can do).

```
newTokens.data
    .setVars({'httpResponse': get(1)})
    .then(get(0))
    .then(map(function(req) {
        return { username: req.body.username, password: req.body.password };
    }))
    .then(models.users.findOne.bind(models.users))
    .then(filterWithMessage({code: 404, msg: 'Invalid credentials'}, isNotEmpty))
    .then(function(usr) {
        return jwt.sign({
            name: usr.first_name,
            birth_date: usr.birth_date
        }, SECRET , {"expiresIn": "1 day "});
    })
    .then(map(function(t) { return { token: t }; }))
    .done(toJSONResponse)
    .catch(callErrorHandler);
```

So the transformations are as follows:

1. Map to get the login data from the request.

2. Then it finds the user with that information.

3. Filter out requests that don't return a user from the previous point.

4. Then sign the request with a token that will expire in one day.

5. Turn the return object into a simpler json with only the token information.

6. Print out the response back to the client.

And like I did before, I'm going to take a look at the marble diagram in Figure 4-5.

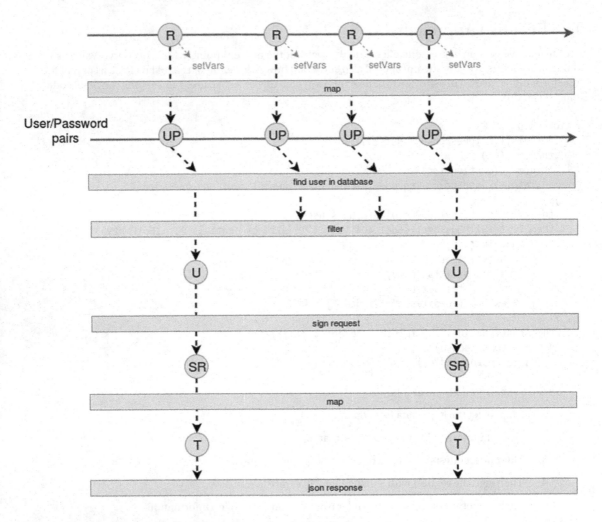

Figure 4-5. *Marble diagram for the reactive authentication logic*

Figure 4-5 is not only showing the ideal path, where all credentials are valid, and there are no errors during the set of transformations, but it is also showing how some requests will be filtered out, due to them not having the right user credentials. The function used to filter out those requests is actually using a simple filter call, with some extra logic:

```
var filterWithMessage = function(opts, fn) {
    var self = this;
    return function(data) {
        var fnFilter = filter(fn );
        if(fnFilter(data) !== null) {
            return data;
        } else {
            return self
                .customVars
                .httpResponse
```

```
        .status(opts.code)
        .json({error: true, msg: opts.msg});
    }
  };
}
```

Thanks to the little framework I'm using, which is modifying the context of the functions I set on the transformation chain, I can directly send the response back to the client from within this function like you can see in the else block from before.

Finally, checking for the actual authenticity of the token received (if received) can be done like I did on the regular approach, simply with an Express middleware, but I can also add that logic as a couple of `filter` steps to the regular chain, and that would allow you to remain independent of the web framework you're using and whether or not it has the middleware capability.

That being said, here's the code that you would have to add:

```
list.data
    .setVars({'httpResponse': get(1), 'next': get(2)})
    .then(get(0))
    .then(filter(function(req) {
        var token = req.query.token || (req.body && req.body.token);
        return !!token;
    }))
    .then(filter(function(req, done ) {
        var token = req.query.token || (req.body && req.body.token);
        jwt.verify(token, SECRET, done);
    }))
    .then(find({}))
    .then(populate('addresses'))
    .then(execute)
    .done(toJSONResponse)
    .catch(callErrorHandler);
```

And here is the code for the filter function, as you can see, it provides two ways to be executed, depending on the number of parameters it receives.

```
function filter(filterFn) {
var fn = null;
if(filterFn.length == 1) {
    fn = function(val) {
        if(filterFn(val)) {
            return val;
        }
        return null;
    };
} else {
    fn = function(val, done) {
        filterFn(val, function(err) {
            if(err) {
                return done(err);
            }
            return done();
        });
    };
```

```
    }
    fn.__type = 'filter';
    return fn;
}
```

The bolded code on the reactive example is what I added, and you can see how I simply added the two checks I had on our middleware from the classic approach, whether or not the token is provided, and then whether or not it is valid. The catch, here, is that even though the request might get filtered, it needs to provide a response to the client, so the request can be closed and the user can understand what's wrong with it. In order to do that, the `filter` function actually calls the function you set using the done method, assuming it's the last function you want to execute on every transformation.

If that doesn't sound too good, there is a second approach, with a fake `filter` like I did before:

```
list.data
    .setVars({'httpResponse': get(1), 'next': get(2)})
    .then(get(0))
    .then(filterWithMessage({code: 401, msg: 'no token provided'}, function(req) {
        var token = req.query.token || (req.body && req.body.token);
        return !!token;
    }))
    .then(filterWithMessage({code: 401, msg: 'unauthorized request'}, function(req, done) {
        var token = req.query.token || (req.body && req.body.token);
        jwt.verify(token, SECRET, done);
    }))
    .then(find({}))
    .then(populate('addresses'))
    .then(execute)
    .done(toJSONResponse)
    .catch(callErrorHandler);
```

In Conclusion

This is another clear example of how the declarative nature of your code allows you to simplify the logic behind it—specifically, to the external reader, someone who isn't the author but needs to understand it. The middleware's code was simple, but yet, it managed to make it more readable by removing the IFs and transforming its logic into two simple `filter` statements. If you think about it, the current approach allowed you to create a filtering middleware without actually looking to implement a middleware. How awesome is that?!

The same can be said for the endpoint's logic—it was simple enough, but with the code, it's much easier to read and understand than before.

Summary

This chapter was all about providing practical evidence that you can use functional reactive programming on the back-end of your applications, and that by doing so, you can improve some aspects of your code, like readability and maintainability.

Hopefully, with the examples provided, that point was made, and you'll be interested in applying these concepts to your own code. That being said, I still need to go over the actual framework's code, which will come in future chapters.

As for the next chapter, I'll go over some of the advantages of using Node.js for a FRP framework.

CHAPTER 5

■ ■ ■

Enter Node.js

Although you already saw how to apply the reactive concepts on the back-end from a practical standpoint, I haven't really talked about how why using Node.js is such a good idea for this.

Instead of looking at code, which you did plenty of in the Chapter 4, in this chapter I'll try to hit the theory aspect of Node. That means I'll take a hard, long look at things like EventEmitters and Streams, and you'll see how asynchronous programming works and why Node.js is so good at it. Finally, asynchronous streams of events, which I already covered a bit in a previous chapter.

By the end of the chapter, you should have a better understanding of the tools provided by Node that will allow you to create the reactive framework I keep promising. Some of these tools will only be mentioned, and some of them will be used in future chapters.

Event Emitters and Event Streams

In this section of the chapter, I'll go over one of the tools that will help you achieve your goal. The EventEmitter module comes native with Node.js since its early versions and will provide you the ability to propagate messages using an event system not different from the one present on browsers (I'm talking about UI events here).

I'll also go over Streams in Node. Just like the EventEmitters, streams are native to Node.js and use some of the things seen on EventEmitters and then add some more magic to provide a very familiar and interesting interface to deal with streams of data.

Event Emitters

An interesting fact about event emitters is that you've probably used them already without even knowing. Some of the core functionalities of Node extend this module and provide you with custom events to listen to. For instance, the *process* object allows you to react to events like uncaughtException, which the server returned by the http module's createServer method, and allows you to listen for special events called request, and so on.

So, what exactly are event emitters? Easily enough, this module will allow you to emit events, but more to the point, it will provide an API for the developer to listen to, react to, and even emit custom events.

Here are some facts about the EventEmitter that might be useful:

- You can set as many listeners to an event as you want.

- When an event is triggered, the listeners are all called one by one and in order, according to the order they were set.

- You can set up the listeners to either be triggered every time the event is received or just the first time.

© Fernando Doglio 2016
F. Doglio, *Reactive Programming with Node.js*, DOI 10.1007/978-1-4842-2152-5_5

- Because of the previous bullet points, there are two ways to add listeners to an event, either by appending them to the list (by using the on, or the once methods) or by prepending them (with either the prependOnceListener method or the prependListener one).

- The listener function doesn't have to have any specific signature to be valid. Any parameter passed to the event during triggering will automatically be passed to this function, in the same order.

- There is a special 'error' event that, when triggered and left without any listeners, will close the node application.

- So in other words, with EventEmitters, you can control the flow of your logic using events, much like you can do on the front-end, when you set up your logic to be initialized after the page is done loading, or like when you setup an AJAX request upon clicking on a link.

- In particular, this mechanic is great when you have an asynchronous process that might need to send back data to the client using it in several occasions mid-process.

For instance, imagine a function that needs to make three different asynchronous requests before finishing, and in mid-process it also needs to report back the progress after finishing each internal request. You can easily do this with the help of EventEmitters, by emitting a custom progress event to which the client can subscribe. Let's look at a quick example:

```
var EventEmitter  = require("events"),
      request = require("request"),
      async = require("async");

function myAsyncEmitter() {}

myAsyncEmitter.prototype = new EventEmitter();

myAsyncEmitter.prototype.process = function() {
      var self = this;
      var doneRequests = 0;

      var urls = [
              "http://www.google.com",
              "http://www.youtube.com",
              "http://www.facebook.com"
      ];

      async.map(urls, function(url, done) {
              request.get(url, function(err, data) {
                      doneRequests++;
                      self.emit('progress', (doneRequests / urls.length) * 100);
                      done(err, data.body);
              });
      }, function(err, results) {
              self.emit('done', results);
      });
};
```

```
var AE = new myAsyncEmitter();
AE.on('progress', function(percentage) {
        console.log("Percentage done: ", percentage, "%");
});

AE.once('done', function(data) {
        console.log("Process over, this is the data: ", data);
});

AE.process();
```

■ **Note**   To simplify the code, I'm using the Async.js and Request.js (available from `https://github.com/request/request`) libraries to provide helper functions that will help you handle the asynchronous calls and the actual requests. They are not required to test the EventEmitter; it is simply a matter of keeping the focus on the interesting bit, which in this case is the Event Emitter.

The previous code is a basic example of what I mentioned before, my custom emitter is extending Node's Event module, to gain access to the desired logic and then I'm using it by setting up the listeners for both events, progress and done. Because I know the done event will be called only once, I set the listener using the once method, but of course, it could've been done with the on method; in this case it would've made no difference (it's merely a measure to increase code readability).

Streams

Like the Event Emitters, Streams are native constructs provided by Node.js and are often either left unused by developers or misunderstood. And just like with EventEmitters, you've probably used more than one stream already and didn't even notice.

So in this section, I want to go over the module and show how it relates to both the EventEmitters seen earlier and the overall goal of this book. Hopefully you'll find similarities between what I've shown you so far and this.

There are four types of streams available from this module:

- *Readable streams*: will provide the API to read data from a given source.

- *Writable streams*: will allow you to write continues chunks of data to a given destination.

- *Duplex streams*: a combination of Readable and Writable streams, allowing you to both write to and read from a given source.

- *Transform streams*: a kind of duplex streams that allow you to transform the data while reading it and writing it.

Each stream also has two modes, one in which you can read and write any JavaScript type (except for null) called Object Mode, and the default one, in which anything passing through a stream is either a String or a Buffer. So if my math is right, we have the total of eight different streams to choose, so I'll dive a little deeper into each one to show the API they provide and how you would have to go about implementing each type of stream.

Readable Streams

Readable streams allow you to wrap a given source of data into a standard API that will let you consume the information provided, either by manually pooling the source or simply by reacting to its arrival.

There are several very common readable streams that developers use almost daily, for instance:

- HTTP response objects on the client side (meaning any application that connects to your API)

- HTTP request objects on the server side

- TCP sockets

- Child process `stdin` and `stderr`

- Etc.

All the different streams provide a set of methods or events that we can use to either read or write the data. In the case of a readable stream, it will either emit a 'data' event every time there is a new chunk of data (or a new object available, depending on whether we're on Object more or not) or you can pipe the output of the reader into a writable stream. The latter gives you no control over what's going on, you simply plug the output of one stream to the input of another, and the system takes care of the rest for you.

Here is a simple example of *piping*. The following code will connect three different streams together:

```
var fs = require("fs"),
    zlib = require("zlib");
var r = fs.createReadStream('file.txt');

var z = zlib.createGzip();

var w = fs.createWriteStream('file.txt.gz');

r.pipe(z).pipe(w);
```

The previous code is creating three different streams and piping them together in the last line. The end result will be the ability to zip a given file and save it to disk.

Simply to show the equivalent code when doing it without piping, here is how you would go about it:

```
var fs = require("fs"),
    zlib = require("zlib");

var r2 = fs.createReadStream('file.txt');
var z2 = zlib.createGzip();
var w2 = fs.createWriteStream('file.txt.gz');

w2.on('open', function() {
        r2.on('data', function(chunk) {
                console.log("data chunk: ", chunk);
                z2.write(chunk);
        });

        z2.on('data', function(data) {
                console.log("-- gzip chunk --");
                w2.write(data);
        });
```

```
    r2.on('end', function() {
            z2.end();
    });

    z2.on('end', function (){
            w2.end();
    });
});
```

Clearly, the code is a bit longer, and there is more to handle manually, but sometimes that is needed, even if it's just to add some debugging messages like in the previous code.

This code is showing one particular event that is very useful when dealing with readable streams: the data event. This event will be fired every time there is a newly available *chunk* of data ready to be consumed by your code.

Readable streams can also emit the readable event, which happens whenever there are data available to be read. In this case, the consumer would have to call the read method of the stream in order to get that next bit of data. This would come in handy when you require extra layers of control over the behavior of your stream—particularly the previous event would only let you know once new data were received, while this one would let you decide what to do once data are available and before they are actually received (depending on your logic, you could read it or ignore it).

There are other useful, though simpler, events emitted by readable streams, such as the end event, emitted to notify that there are no more data to be read; the close event, emitted once there are no more events to emit; and the error event, which I already covered.

Writable Streams

In the case of writable streams, they work just like the opposite of readable streams: They wrap the destination of your data into an easy-to-use container. And just like with any other stream, you can pipe other streams to it, or you can manually write to it.

Some common writable streams are:

- fs write streams

- zlib streams (like you saw above)

- crypto streams

Using these streams is pretty straightforward. The main methods you'll want to know about are write to actually send data to it and end to close it. I've already shown how they work on the previous code sample, so I'm not going to bore you with them again.

Since all streams are also EventEmitters, they will trigger some specific events. In the case of the writables, you should pay special attention to:

- *drain*: This event is triggered after a stream.write call returns false. Once this event is triggered, then the writing can be resumed. This event can be triggered by your stream when the destination of your writes has been overwhelmed and needs some time before the next chunk of data can be sent.

- *error*: This one is common to all EventEmitters, so please, whenever you're creating a stream, set a handler for this event; otherwise, your entire application will crash if this error is not handled.

Duplex and Transform Streams

These two types of streams are actually based on the previous two. You have the Duplex stream, which is simply (and obviously) a stream that implements both the Readable and the Writable interfaces (like a TCP socket).

And then you have the Transform streams, which are Duplex streams, but with the variation that allows you to change the input it receives into something else before it becomes the output. In other words, you could, for instance, create a Transform stream that receives JavaScript Objects and writes JSON strings into some storage system.

The main difference between a Duplex and a Transform stream, aside from the obvious, of course, is that for the Duplex stream, the Read and Write events are being handled in parallel of each other, meaning individually. The Write action/event is not tied to the Read that one would expect to come before, so if you're dealing with asynchronous processes (which in Node.js you most probably will be), take that into account. I'll show you a specific case of this below.

Writing Your Custom Stream

The previous code shows an example of how to use both a premade readable and a premade writable stream, but what it doesn't do is show you how to implement your own custom streams, because let's face it, once you understand streams, you'll want to use them every chance you get! (At least that's what happened to me!)

I provide a very simple example here to show how easy is it to create objects that comply with the descriptions of each type of stream.

The following code will set up an endpoint on an HTTP server that receives data and through a set of streams. It will:

- Get the body of the request and transform it into a JavaScript object.

- Add one attribute to it.

- Save it to a database.

- Transform it back into a String.

- Return the string back to the client.

```
var  inherits = require("util").inherits;
var streams = require("stream");
var Transform = streams.Transform;

//Turns the request's body into an object
function GetBody() {
    Transform.call(this, {objectMode: true});
}

inherits(GetBody, Transform);

GetBody.prototype._transform = function(obj, encoding, callback) {
    var str = obj.toString();
    callback(null, JSON.parse(str));
};
```

```
//Adds the timestamp value
function AddTimeStamp() {
    Transform.call(this, {objectMode: true});
}

inherits(AddTimeStamp, Transform);

AddTimeStamp.prototype._transform = function(obj, encoding, callback) {
    obj.timestamp = Date.now();
    callback(null, obj);
};

//Turns the object into a string
function ToJSONEncoder() {
    Transform.call(this, {objectMode: true});
}

inherits(ToJSONEncoder, Transform);

ToJSONEncoder.prototype._transform = function(obj, encoding, callback) {
    callback(null, JSON.stringify(obj));
};

//Saves the object into the database
function SaveUserToDB() {
    Transform.call(this, {objectMode: true});
}

inherits(SaveUserToDB, Transform);

SaveUserToDB.prototype._transform = function(obj, encoding, callback) {
    var self = this;
    UserModel.create(obj, function(err, obj) {
        if(err) {
            return callback(err);
        }
        self.push(obj);
        callback();
    });
};

var addTimeStamp = new AddTimeStamp();
var save = new SaveUserToDB();
var getBody = new GetBody();
var toJSON = new ToJSONEncoder();
```

```
function handleNewUsers(req, res, next) {
        req
            .pipe(getBody)
            .pipe(addTimeStamp)
            .pipe(save)
            .pipe(toJSON)
            .pipe(res);
}
```

As you can see, you can do all that by creating a set of Transform streams and leveraging the fact that the Request object is also a ReadableStream and that the Response object is a WritableStream by default on Node.

If you want to test this code, you'll also need the setup code that comes before it, so here it is (and, of course, you'll need this to install the dependencies like MongoDB, mongoose and express):

```
var mongoose = require("mongoose");
var express = require("express");

// --- db
var Schema = mongoose.Schema;

var UserSchema = Schema({
        full_name: String,
        birthdate: Date,
        username: String,
        password: String,
        timestamp: Number
});

var UserModel = mongoose.model("User", UserSchema);

mongoose.connect('mongodb://localhost/test-streams');

//--- http server
var app = express();

app.post('/users', handleNewUsers);

app.listen(3000, function() {
        console.log("Ready to roll!");
});
```

It simply takes care of setting up the HTTP server and the MongoDB connection and defining the schema for the model.

■ **Caution**   When writing code that uses the stream properties of the Request object like the previous one, refrain from using the body-parse (available at https://www.npmjs.com/package/body-parser) middleware module for Express, because it will affect it, and your code will not work.

Finally, I'd like to draw your attention to the SaveUserToDB stream, which originally I thought of as a Duplex stream. It would write the object into the database and then return it on the following Read call, but as it turns out, due to what I described earlier (when talking about Duplex v Transform streams), the Read and Write events are not linked, so I would get the Read event before the Write was done and therefore I would have nothing to return at that point. This is solved by turning the Stream into a Transform stream.

A good example of when a Duplex stream would come in handy would be some kind of client/server connection handler—basically a stream that would let you write messages from the server to the client and at the same time read the messages received by the server on the client application.

In the end, when trying to implement a custom stream, Table 5-1 will help you understand which methods need to be implemented and when.

Table 5-1. *Simple Cheatsheet to Explain When to Implement What Kind of Stream*

When Doing...	Your Stream Is a...	And You Have to Implement...
Reads only	Readable	_read
Writes only	Writable	_write
Reads and Writes	Duplex	_read, _write
Changes to the data you write	Transform	_transform

Asynchronous Programming in Node.js

So far, I've talked about using asynchronous functions almost everywhere, but I haven't really given an explanation on what that is. So let's talk about that, shall we?

Asynchronous (or Async) programming is probably one of the best and, at the same time, most confusing features of Node.js.

What asynchronous programming means, put simply, is that for every asynchronous function that you execute, it will not return the results before moving forward with the program's flow. Instead, you'll need to provide a callback function that will be executed once the asynchronous code finishes.

Figure 5-1 shows what would be a regular, non-asynchronous flow.

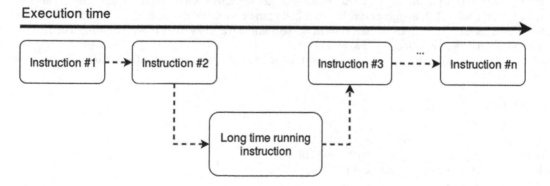

Figure 5-1. *Simple example of a synchronous flow*

Figure 5-1 represents a set of instructions that run in a synchronous manner. It is clear that in order to execute Instruction #4, it needs to wait as long as the long time running instruction takes and then wait for Instruction #3 to finish. But what if Instruction #4 and #3 weren't really related? What if you didn't really mind in which order Instruction #3 and #4 executed in relationship to each other?

Then you could put the long time running instruction to be executed in an asynchronous manner and provide Instruction #3 as a callback to that, allowing you to execute Instruction #4 much sooner.

Figure 5-2 shows how that would look.

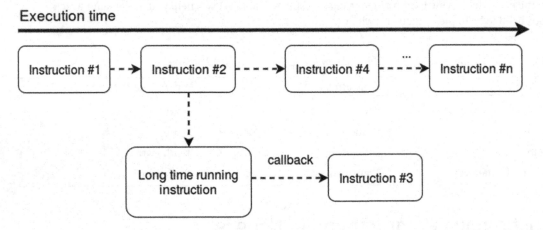

Figure 5-2. *Example of an asynchronous flow*

Instruction #4 is executed right after Instruction #2 starts the asynchronous long time running instruction, instead of waiting for it to finish.

That is, of course, a very simple example of the potential benefits of asynchronous programming. It is not always possible to use this approach either. You can do this with I/O bound functions, because that's how Node.js handles I/O (I'll discuss this in a bit, don't worry), but CPU bound functions, like heavy number crunching, will not really work this way and they will block the flow just like a synchronous function would, so take that into account when planning your code.

Finally, like with most in this digital world, nothing comes without a price, and the added benefits also come with a nasty trade off: debugging asynchronous code can be a real head-breaker.

Developers are trained to think of their code in the sequential way they write it, so debugging a code that is not sequential can be difficult to newcomers.

For instance, let's look at the same piece of code both written in synchronous and asynchronous manner:

Synchronous version:

```
var fs = require("fs");
console.log("About to read the file... ");
var content = fFs .readFileSync("/path/to/file");
console.log("File content: ", content) ;
```

Asynchronous version (with a common mistake):

```
var fs = require("fs");
console.log("About to read the file...");
var content = "";
```

```
fs.readFile("/path/to/file", function(err, data) {
    content = data;
});
console.log("File content: ", content);
```

If you haven't guessed it yet, the second code will print:

```
File content:
```

And the reason for that is directly related to the diagram from before. Figure 5-3 shows what's going on with the buggy asynchronous version.

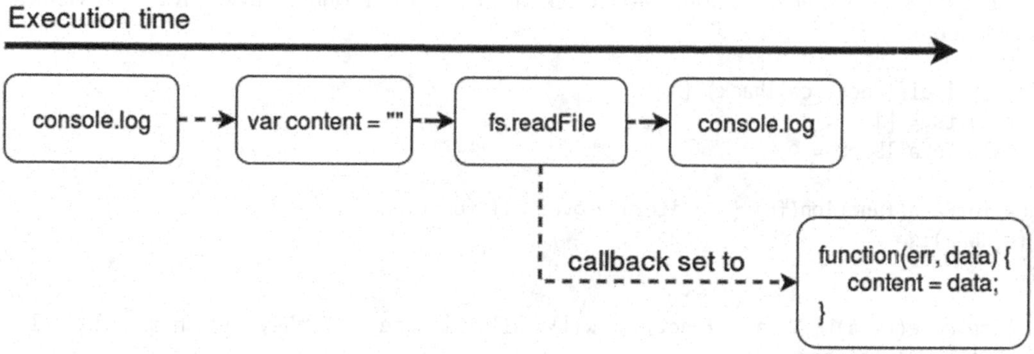

Execution time

Figure 5-3. *A classic asynchronous programming mistake*

It's pretty clear by looking at Figure 5-3 why the content of the file is not getting written, because the callback is being executed after the last console.log line. This is a very common mistake done by new developers, not only with node.js but, more specifically, with AJAX calls on the front-end. They set up their code in a way where they try to use the content returned by the asynchronous call before it actually ends.

So to finish with the example, let's look at how the code would have to be written in order to properly work:

```
var fs = require("fs");
console.log("About to read the file...");
var content = "";
fs.readFile("/path/to/file", function(err, data) {
    content = data;
    console.log("File content: ", content);
});
```

Simple, just moved the last console.log line into the callback function, so you're sure the content variable is set correctly.

Async Advanced

Asynchronous programming is not just about making sure you set up the callback function correctly, it also allows for some interesting flow control patterns that can be used to improve the efficiency of the app.

Let's look at two distinct and very useful control flow patterns for asynchronous programming: *parallel flow* and *serial flow*.

Parallel Flow

The idea behind parallel flow is that the program can run a set of non-related tasks in parallel but only call the callback function provided (to gather their collective outputs) after all tasks have finished executing.

Basically, this is what I'm talking about:

```
//functionX symbols are references to individual functions
parallel([function1, function2, function3, function4], function(data) {
    ///do something with the combined output once they all finished
})
```

In order to know when each of the functions have finished execution, they'll have to execute a callback function with the results of their operation. The callback will be the only attribute they receive, so let's look at the parallel function:

```
function parallel(funcs, callback) {
    var results = [],
        callsToCallback = 0;

    funcs.forEach(function(fn) { // iterate over all functions
        fn(done);
    });

    function done(data) { // the functions will call this one when they finish and they'll
      pass the results here
        results.push(data);
        if(++callsToCallback == funcs.length) {
            callback(results);
        }
    }
}
```

■ **Note** Because of the asynchronous nature of the functions called during the execution of `parallel`, the order of the results on the final callback can't be assured. Some of the asynchronous functions that execute at the beginning might take longer to return results than the ones executed later. Extra code would be needed to ensure that the final list of results is sorted.

The previous implementation is a very simple version of what I'm trying to demonstrate, but it fulfills its task: It runs a set of functions in a parallel-like way (you'll see that since Node.js runs in a single thread, true parallelism is not possible, so this is as close as we can get).

This type of control flow is particularly useful when dealing with calls to external services.

Let's look at a practical example: Assume your program needs to do several operations that, despite not being related to each other, need to happen before the user can see the results. For instance, load the list of books from the database, query an external service to get news from new books out this week, and log the request into a file. If you were to execute all those tasks in a series, waiting for one to finish before the next one can be run, then the user would most probably suffer a delay on the response, since the total time needed for the execution would be the sum of all individual times.

But if instead you can execute all of them in parallel, then the total time would actually equal the time it took to the slowest task to execute[1].

Let's look at both cases:

Serial way (takes longer)

```
//request handling code...
//assume "db" is already initialized and provides an interface to the data base
db.query("books", {limit:1000, page: 1}, function(books) {
  services.bookNews.getThisWeeksNews(function(news) {
    services.logging.logRequest(request, function() { //nothing returned, but we need to
    call it so we know the logging finished
      response.render({listOfBooks: books, bookNews: news})
    })
  })
})
```

Parallel way (takes a lot less time)

```
//request handling code...
parallel([
  function(callback) { db.query("books", {limit: 1000, page: 1}, callback) }),
  function(callback) { services.bookNews.getThisWeeksNews(callback) }),
  function(callback) { services.logRequest(request, callback) })
], function(data) {
    var books = findData('books', data)
    var news = findData('news', data)
    response.render({listOfBooks: books, bookNews: news})
})
```

The preceding code shows how each approach would look. The findData function simply looks into the data array and, based on the structure of the items, returns the desired one (first parameter). In this implementation of parallel it is needed because (as I mentioned before) you can't be sure in which order the functions finished and sent their results back.

Aside from the clear speed boost that the code will get, it's also easier to read and easier to add new tasks to the parallel flow: Just add a new item to the array.

Serial Flow

The serial flow provides the means to easily specify a list of functions that need to be executed in a particular order. This solution doesn't provide a speed boost, like the previous one did, but it does provide the ability to write such code and keep it clean, staying away from what is normally known as callback hell.

Let's look at what we're trying to accomplish:

```
serial([
 function1, function2, function3
], function(data) {
   //do something with the combined results
});
```

---

[1]This is of course a rough approximation, since the time added by the parallel function needs to be taken into account for an exact number.

Instead of having something like:

```
function1(function(data1)  {
    function2(function(data2) {
     function3(function(data3) {
       //do something with all the output
     }
   }
}
```

You can see how the second piece of code can get out of hand if the number of functions keeps growing. So the serial approach will help you keep the code organized and readable.

Let's look at a possible implementation of the serial function:

```
function serial(functions, done) {
    var fn = functions.shift(); //get the first function off the list

    var results = [];
    fn(next);

    function next(result) {
        results.push(result); //save the results to be passed into the final callback once
        we don't have any more functions to execute.
        var nextFn = functions.shift();
        if (nextFn) nextFn(next);
        else done(results);
    }
}
```

There are more variations to these functions, like using an error parameter to handle errors automatically or limiting the number of simultaneous functions on the parallel flow.

All in all, asynchronous programming is an integral part of the Node.js developer's life. Everything takes advantage of Node's asynchronous I/O (which I'll talk about in a minute), so understanding how it works and how you can leverage its power in your favor will definitely help you when designing the reactive library.

For a fully functional and tested library that thrives on asynchronous programming, please check out ASYNC.JS (available at `https://github.com/caolan/async`).

Asynchronous I/O

A specific case of Asynchronous programming relates to this very interesting feature provided by Node.js: Asynchronous I/O.

This feature is highly related to the internal architecture of Node.js. As I've said before, Node doesn't provide multithreading; it actually works with a single thread inside which it runs an event loop (see Figure 5-4).

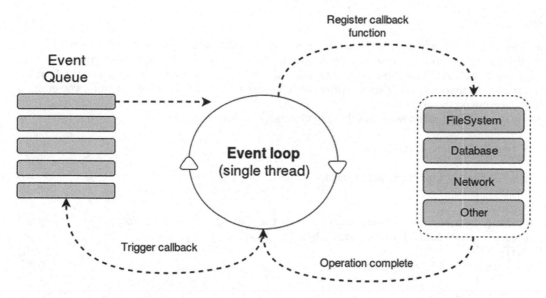

Figure 5-4. *Diagram showing how the Event Loop works to provide Async I/O*

In a nutshell, Node.js was designed with the mindset that I/O operations are the actual bottleneck on every operation, not the processing power, so every request received by the node process will work inside the event loop until an I/O operation is found. When that happens, the callback will be registered on a separate queue, and the main program's flow will continue. Once the I/O operation finishes, the callback will be triggered and the code inside it will be run.

Asynchronous Streams of Events

The heading could also be Streams of Asynchronous events. Either way, the point of this section of the chapter is to tie together everything I've talked about so far.

In Chapter 3 I showed some basic code on how to handle this type of situation, and it works, but since Node already provides native Streams, it's important to go over all options, so that in the future chapters, you can draw from these different options and create a great library.

For the purpose of this demonstration, I'll use an external module called *event-stream* (available at https://www.npmjs.com/package/event-stream), but don't worry, it uses Node's built-in streams as the basis of everything, so it still applies.

This library basically provides a set of helper methods that will let you manipulate and deal with streams that, in turn, can easily deal with asynchronous tasks. If you remember from a few pages ago, the SaveUserToDB stream could not be made a Duplex stream, instead I had to go with a Transform stream, because of the asynchronous call to the database.

Well, with the help of the event-stream module, fixing this is not only simple, but there are actually a couple of ways to do it. Let's first look at all the helper methods provided by the library.

Through

This method is the solution to the problem from before. It creates a Duplex stream on which we can control the flow of data, allowing you to turn an asynchronous process into a synchronous one. It accepts two optional parameters, a write function and an end function. You'll notice that there is no read method, and that is because it's a special kind of Duplex, with a predefined read method. It re-emits whatever you emit with the data event on the write method.

Let me show you. Here is how the SaveUserToDB stream can be re-written:

```
var es = require("event-stream");

var save = es.through(function write(data) {
    var self = this;
    this.pause();
    //You need to pause the stream, to make sure the saving operation is done
    UserModel.create(data, function(err, obj) {
        if(err) {
            return self.emit('error', err);
        }
        self.resume();
        //you can then resume the stream and emit the new object
        self.emit('data', obj);
    });
}, function end() {
    this.emit('end');
});
```

Map

This method accepts two parameters: the actual data and a callback function that *must* be called at the end of the function.

I've covered what the map function does in a previous chapter, so in this case it should be enough to understand that this particular map, is a custom through function that re-emits whatever you send as the second parameter of the received callback. So knowing this, you can re-implement the SaveUserToDB stream yet again, like so:

```
var es = require("event-stream");

var save = es.map(function(data, callback) {
    var self = this;
    UserModel.create(data, function(err, obj) {
        if(err) {
            //the first argument of the callback is the error returned
            return callback(err);
        }
        callback(null, obj);
    });
});
```

Split

This method works similarly to how the `String#split` method works, but its default value is the end-of-line character instead of the empty string. Instead of splitting a single string, this method will break up a stream and reassemble it, so that every part of the resulting split, is a chunk of data.

An easy example for this would be if you wanted to process each word of a text document, you could do something like the following:

```
var es = require("event-stream");

var fs = require("fs");

fs.createReadStream('myfile.txt')
        .pipe(es.split(' '))
        .pipe(es.map(function(word, cb) {
                cb(null, word.toUpperCase());
        });
```

Clearly you don't need to split a document into words to do just that, but it serves as an example nonetheless.

Join

This one is a bit confusing, because the name would suggest that it is the opposite of split, which would allow you to undo whatever you did with it.

This adds a separator (the only attribute it accepts) after each chunk emitted, so in practice, for every bit of data, it is emitting two new ones, the separator and the actual data. So you can do something like the following:

```
var es = require("event-stream");

var fs = require("fs");

var writer = fs.createWriteStream('./output-join.txt');

fs.createReadStream('./event-stream-join.js')

        .pipe(es.split(" "))

        .pipe(es.map(function(str, done) {

                done(null, str.toUpperCase());

        }))

        .pipe(es.join("\n"))

        .pipe(writer);
```

Effectively the code above is splitting a text file into words, making each word uppercase and then saving each word into a file but with a new-line character at the end.

■ **Tip** If instead of passing in a String as parameter to the join method, you pass in a function, then that function will be called once the stream ends, and the only parameter it will receive will be the list of chunks emitted but all concatenated as a single String.

Merge

This method takes care of merging several streams, and that means that it will merge the resulting data from each of the passed streams, and once all of them have issued the end event, then it will end.

A simple example of this would be:

```
var es = require("event-stream");

var fs = require("fs");

es.merge([

  fs.createReadStream('input1.txt'),

  fs.createReadStream('input2.txt')

]).pipe(fs.createWriteStream('output.log'));
```

Note that no ordering is ensured between the merged streams, so the saved data will not have the content of one file first, and the second later. The content of both files could be intertwined (depending on how lengthy the content of each file is).

Readable

As the name of this method indicates, it creates a Readable stream, one that works with an asynchronous function as source of data. In other words, the function received (the only parameter accepted) accepts two arguments: a counter and a callback. The function must always call the callback in order to advance the flow of data, and it can only call it once; further calls will have no effect.

It can, however, emit several chunks of data in a single call, using the data event. Here is the basic structure of your read function:

```
var es = require("event-stream");

es.readable(function(count, callback) {
        if(hasEnded) { //for some reason the stream is no longer reading
                this.emit('end');
        }

        //... your code here
        this.emit('data', chunk); //you can do this as many times as you need to.
        callback();
});
```

> ■ **Note** In the preceding code example, the variable hasEnded is merely a placeholder for some kind of logical condition that indicates the stream has ended. You would need to replace it with whatever makes sense to your business logic.

There are other methods provided by the module, like duplex, child, wait, parse, etc., but the main ones are the ones from earlier. If you wish to know more, you can check the full documentation on the module's npm page (available at https://www.npmjs.com/package/event-stream).

In Conclusion

As you can see, the helper methods provided by this module are very similar to those described in Chapter 3 but, at the same time, different in the sense that they create new streams instead of modifying the data flowing through one.

This module and the Observable Streams discussed before will be used to create the final version of this book's reactive library.

Summary

Hopefully this chapter has shed some light on a very misunderstood and often forgotten feature of Node.js.

Built-in streams will be a great tool when dealing with reactive code on the back-end, like you've seen in past chapters. So now that you know how to use them you can start tinkering yourself!

The next chapter will cover the main libraries out there that deal specifically with reactive programming in JavaScript—particularly in Node.js.

CHAPTER 6

■ ■ ■

Overview of the Land

So far, in this book I've covered what reactive programming (RP) is, how useful it can be on the back end, and, finally, how Node.js is such a great match for it. I even went ahead and showed some code alternatives on how to accomplish a reactive back end.

In this chapter, before I go deep into the creation of this book's reactive library, I want to go over the current libraries out there. Some of them are not really meant for Node.js, and some of them are, but the important thing here is that it's all JavaScript and you might end up learning from them, even though they can't really be used as they are being used on the back end.

By the end of this chapter, you should have all you need to start getting your hands dirty with the code for the reactive library that's coming up.

Reactive Extension for JavaScript: RxJS

Also known as the Reactive Extension for JavaScript (please look at `http://reactivex.io/`), RxJS is, as of this writing, in version 4.0 and it's one of the most popular reactive libraries out there.

This project is actively developed by Microsoft, but there is a huge open source community behind it as well, helping improve the library. For such contributions, they do provide a Wiki page in case you're interested (which you can find at `https://github.com/Reactive-Extensions/RxJS/wiki/Contributions`). But bear in mind that by the looks of it, they are the only ones who get to decide which features are good for the "product" and which aren't, so bug fixes and documentation improvements are welcomed; new features, however, will have to be discussed before even considering them. This is probably due to the fact that Rx is a suite of libraries for multiple languages, all based on the same principles, so adding a new feature to one would imply adding that same feature to the rest of them.

Another benefit of it being backed by such a big organization is that this library has a huge amount of documentation behind it. I'm not just talking about online tutorials, there are also several books and workshops available too. You can get the full list of resources from their Github page (`https://github.com/Reactive-Extensions/RxJS#resources`).

License

This library is distributed under the Apache License, version 2.0 (`http://www.apache.org/licenses/LICENSE-2.0`), which basically means you can use it for commercial products without a problem and you can modify it and distribute it, but if you do, you'll have to include a list of the changes you made and a copy of the license as well. So all in all, you're pretty much free to do whatever you want with it, as long as you comply with some basic rules.

© Fernando Doglio 2016
F. Doglio, *Reactive Programming with Node.js*, DOI 10.1007/978-1-4842-2152-5_6

Compatibility

RxJS is compatible with all major browsers all the way back to some pretty scary versions—to be more specific, Internet Explorer 6+, Firefox 1.0+, and Chrome 4+. Hopefully you're not really using such archaic versions of these browsers, but just in case.

Amazingly enough, this library is also compatible with Node.js, from version 0.4 and above, so the code samples I'll show will be tested directly in Node (woohoo!).

Code Samples

About those samples, since this is actually Node-compatible, that's what I'll use for them. The first code sample is something pretty basic to get you started.

■ **Note**   In order to use RxJS with Node, you'll have to install the rx package and the node-rx bindings using the classic npm install command: $npm install rx and $npm install node-rx.

```
var rx = require("rx");
var rxnode = require("rx-node") ;

var subscription = rxnode.fromReadableStream(process.stdin);

subscription.filter(function(line) {
        var matches = line.toString().match(/[a]{1}/g);
    return matches !== null && matches.length > 5;
})
.subscribe(function (x) {
        console.log(x.toString());
});
```

As you can see, the Node.js bindings are compatible with Node's streams (check out Chapter 5 if you want to know more about those). In this case I'm simply using the stdin stream, which I can subscribe to after setting up a simple filtering function. In other words, the earlier code will let you enter a sentence, and once you hit enter (which is when the 'data' event of the stdin stream is triggered) it will count the number of A's on it. If it's higher than 5, then it'll print the line again; otherwise it will do nothing.

The code might be simple, but it's enough to get you started. Basically you'll always be following the same pattern:

- Find a stream to use.

- Configure a set of transformations/operations on the data of the stream.

- Finally, subscribe to the stream, passing a final function to use, which will receive the final version of the data chunk sent with the 'data' event.

■ **Tip**   If you're using a custom stream with custom events, you can pass the end event name and the data event name (in that order) to the fromStream method after the actual stream.

Let's look at one more example. This is the re-write of an example from Chapter 5, where the script would read a file as a stream and split it into words, change those words so they're all in capital letters, and then print the words out on a new line for each word.

```
var rx = require("rx");
var noderx = require("rx-node");
var fs = require("fs");

var stream = noderx.fromStream(fs.createReadStream('./test-rxjs2.js'));

stream
    .flatMap(function(s){ return s.toString().split(" ")  })
    .map(function(str) {
        return str.toUpperCase();
    })
    .subscribe(function(b) {
        console.log(b.toString());
    });
```

Because RxJs has no helper methods like the ones provided by the event-stream (remember the split method?) module, in order to split the lines and make the words the new chunks of data on the stream, I used the flatMap method. This method takes the returned value from its function, which might be an Observable or something that can be made an Observable (such as an Array in our case), and flattens it and returns a stream that emits chunks of this new item.

Bacon.js

Bacon.js is a nice little library for doing Functional Reactive Programming in JavaScript. As of this writing, its version is 0.7.84 and although the number might give you the wrong idea (it being pre-version 1 and all), it's been around for over 3 years now and it's quite popular. It's downloaded over 14,000 times each month according to NPM's stats, and in Github (https://github.com/baconjs/bacon.js) it has over 5,000 stars.

It's not clearly stated who the main author of this library is, although after a bit of digging it appears to be Mr. Juha Paananen. You can find a list of active contributors on Github (https://github.com/orgs/baconjs/people). Its documentation appears to be quite comprehensive; they list quite a few resources, like tutorials and even a video example (https://github.com/baconjs/bacon.js/wiki/Documentation).

And finally, if you feel like you need to ask a question, they do have an active Google Group for you (https://groups.google.com/forum/?fromgroups#!forum/baconjs) and an active chat room at Gitter (https://gitter.im/baconjs/bacon.js).

License

In the case of Bacon.js, the license is one of the most permissive ones out there: MIT License. It basically states that you can do pretty much anything with it as long as you properly add a copyright notice and add a copy of the license.

Compatibility

According to its author, the library doesn't really mess with the prototype of existing objects on the language, except in two specific cases:

- On a browser environment, it adds the Bacon object to the `window` instance.

- If jQuery is defined, it adds the method `asEventStream` to it.

With that in mind, the library should be quite compatible with anything else you're using in your project.

As for browser and Node's version compatibility, it's been tested with all major browsers on all modern versions (as stated on Bacon's readme file) and it works with all of them, because it doesn't use any browser-dependent feature. Same thing for Node, since it doesn't use anything from the actual browser, this library is pure JavaScript, which makes it compatible with Node as well.

Code Samples

In the case of Bacon.js, you won't need an extra library with Node.js bindings because like I already mentioned earlier, this library is 100% environment-agnostic JavaScript. That being said, here's a simple example showing how easy it is to create new streams from custom events:

```
var bacon = require("baconjs");
var fs = require("fs");

process.stdin.resume();
process.stdin.setEncoding('utf8');
var util = require('util');

function readFilenames(sink) {
    process.stdin.on('data', function (text) {
        sink(text.trim());
    });
}

//Create a new EventStream from a custom function
var filenames = bacon.fromBinder(readFilenames);

filenames.onValue(function(name) { //tap into the stream to know what's going on
    console.log("-- New filename: ", name, " --");
})

var names = filenames.scan([], function(acc, name) { //grab 2 filenames at a time
    return acc.length === 2 ? [name] : acc.concat(name);
});

var groupfilenames = names.filter(function(acc) { //once we have 2 move on, otherwise, stop here
    return acc.length === 2;
})
.flatMap(bacon.fromArray); //turn the new array into a stream
```

```
groupfilenames.onValue(function(fnames) {
    console.log('[', fnames, ']');
});

groupfilenames.flatMap(function(name) {
    return bacon.fromNodeCallback(fs.readFile, name);
});

.onValue(function(content) {
    //print out the content of the files
    console.log(content.toString());
});
```

■ **Tip**   Installing Bacon.js on your Node.js project is quite simple. All you need is to issue the following command: $ npm install baconjs

---

The preceding code lets the user enter two filenames, then those names are transformed into the actual content of those files. This is all achieved by a series of transformations:

- A stream is created using the fromBinder method, so that every time the user hits ENTER a new chunk of data is emitted (a new filename).

- Then using the scan method, I group the chunks on groups of two.

- By filtering groups that have less than two elements, I'm essentially stopping the flow of data through the stream until each group has two filenames.

- The first flatMap method coupled with the result of fromArray will turn each array into a new stream, which will emit the filenames, but of course, this new stream will have a limited amount of events (only two!).

- Finally, the second flatMap method will turn the asynchronous callback of the fs.readFile method into a stream, making it possible for you to read the content of each file within your stream.

So you can see what I mean on each step, I've added intermediate calls to the onValue method. Figure 6-1 represents the output of the script and it will show you how each stream is affected by the transformations applied to it.

```
file1.txt                                          ──────────────────  User input
-- New filename:  file1.txt  --
file2.txt                           ──────────────────
-- New filename:  file2.txt  --                              User input
[ file1.txt ]
[ file2.txt ]
this is file #1

this is file #2
```

Figure 6-1. *Output from executing the preceding code*

Figure 6-1 shows the output from executing the script. You can see where the user inputs the filenames and what happens in between and after as well.

Let's look at one more example before leaving this library behind. The following code shows how easy it is to grab a single common source of data, split it into several streams, and then merge them together.

```
var fs = require("fs");
var bacon = require("baconjs");

var freadStream = fs.createReadStream("file3.txt");

function readFile(sink) {
    freadStream.on('data', function(chunk) {
        sink(chunk);
    });
}

var fstream = bacon.fromBinder(readFile);
var charStream = fstream.map(function(chunk) {
    return chunk.toString().split("");
}).flatMap(bacon.fromArray);

var onlyNumbers = charStream.filter(function(v) {
    return !isNaN(+v);
});

var onlyChars = charStream.filter(function(v) {
    return isNaN(+v);
});

var all = onlyNumbers.merge(onlyChars);

onlyNumbers
.onValue(function(n) {
    console.log("#", n);
});

onlyChars
.onValue(function(c) {
    console.log("'", c, "'");
});

all
.scan([], function(acc, c) {
    return acc.concat(c);
})
.onValue(function(a) {
    console.log("-", a, "-");
});
```

The code is very simple, but the potential behind it is what matters in this case. You could transform each stream individually and then merge them back together. In the preceding code, the merge is actually done into an array, so the result will be an ever-growing array of value. Figure 6-2 shows the output of the execution.

```
- [] -
' a '
- [ 'a' ] -
' a '
- [ 'a', 'a' ] -
' a '
- [ 'a', 'a', 'a' ] -
# 1
- [ 'a', 'a', 'a', '1' ] -
# 2
- [ 'a', 'a', 'a', '1', '2' ] -
# 3
- [ 'a', 'a', 'a', '1', '2', '3' ] -
# 4
- [ 'a', 'a', 'a', '1', '2', '3', '4' ] -
' a '
- [ 'a', 'a', 'a', '1', '2', '3', '4', 'a' ] -
' a '
- [ 'a', 'a', 'a', '1', '2', '3', '4', 'a', 'a' ] -
' a '
- [ 'a', 'a', 'a', '1', '2', '3', '4', 'a', 'a', 'a' ] -
```

Figure 6-2. *Output from executing the preceding code*

Highland.js

This library (http://highlandjs.org) is a more generic utility module, created by Caolan McMahon (https://twitter.com/caolan) and it's similar in some ways to UnderscoreJS (http://underscorejs. org/) and AsyncJS (http://caolan.github.io/async/, which he created as well) but built on top of Node-like streams, which basically allows it to handle both synchronous and asynchronous code easily.

One of the main features advertised by this library is the so-called "back pressure," which works great with streams that can't be paused. Normally, when the client consuming the stream can't handle more data, it will pause it until it's ready. When the source stream can't be paused, Highland will buffer the data for you until you're ready to resume normal operations.

With regard to documentation, Highland is probably the weakest of the ones discussed here. Although it has a very comprehensive help section on its main website, they don't really list external resources like tutorials, videos, or even books, instead you're left to browse the Internet and find those yourself. The only issue with that is that you never know if those resources are up-to-date or not.

License

Just like with RxJS, the license for HighlandJS is Apache 2.0, so you're free to do whatever you want with this library as long as you add a list of changes (if any) made by you and add a copy of the license as well.

Compatibility

There is no specific mention as to whether this library is compatible with older browsers like the previous are; it is only stated that it does work on browsers and it's installation includes a browserify-ready version of the library. It is also compatible with Node.js, which is what really matters to you and me (again, there is no mention of a specific version of Node, but let's assume it works on modern version of Node).

Code Samples

One of the main advertised features of Highland.js is the fact you can have the same version of your code work with both synchronous and asynchronous data sources, thus simplifying development.

In the following example, I'll show just that; first I'll use a simple Array as a source for the Stream constructor, and then I'll switch it up with a file on disc, and you'll see how the rest of the code remains the same:

```
var  HL = require("highland");

var source = ['value1', 'value2', 'value3'];

HL(source).map(function(v) {
        console.log("Calls++");
        return v.toUpperCase();
});
```

■ **Tip**   To install HighlandJS simply use the npm command: `$ npm install highland`

Now, if you were to go on and execute the preceding code, something interesting will happen: nothing. You see, the aforementioned example demonstrates something else advertised by Highland.js, and that is the lazy evaluation of streams. The library will not immediately start pulling data from the stream; instead, it will let you define your intentions in regards to the transformations you want to exert on the stream, and then, you can tell it to start consuming said stream.

There are a few methods that do this. In fact, they are: each, done, apply, toArray, pipe and resume.

Here's the same code, but with the extra method call, telling HighlandJS to actually start consuming the stream:

```
var  HL = require("highland");

var source = ['value1', 'value2', 'value3'];

HL(source).map(function(v) {
        console.log("Calls++");
        return v.toUpperCase();
}).toArray(function(arr) {
        console.log(arr);
});
```

The output of the above code is the following:

```
Calls++

Calls++

Calls++

[ 'VALUE1', 'VALUE2', 'VALUE3' ]
```

So as you can see, this time around the source stream was consumed properly thanks to the added toArray call.

Let's now look at what happens if I wanted to use a file as a source, instead of a simple array.

```
var HL = require("highland");
var fs = require("fs");

function getData(fname) {
    return function(push, next) {
        fs.readFile(fname, function(err, data) {
            if(err) push(err);
            else {
                var lines = data.toString().split("\n");
                lines.forEach(function(l) {
                    push(null, l);
                });
                push(null, HL.nil);//HL.nil indicates the end of the stream
                next();
            }
        });
    };
}

HL(getData('./file4.txt')).map(function(v) {
    console.log("Calls++");
    return v.toUpperCase();
}).toArray(function(arr) {
    console.log(arr);
});
```

As you can appreciate, the consuming call of the stream remains the same, but the source of that stream is now a file read asynchronously.

Error handling is quite simple as well; the earlier code will fail if the path to the file is wrong, but using the errors method, you can extract the errors from the stream and create a new one, after executing an error handling function, like so:

```
HL(getData('./file42.txt')).map(function(v) {
    console.log("Calls++");
    return v.toUpperCase();
})
```

```
.errors(function(err, push) {
    if(err.code == 'ENOENT') { //If the file is not found, simply return an empty string so
    the code is not affected
        push(null, '');
    } else {
        push(err);
    }
})
.toArray(function(arr) {
    console.log(arr);
});
```

To continue with the file-reading theme, let's look at another example, similar to what I showed with Bacon.js earlier. This time, I'll have an array of filenames and the code will take those filenames, read each file, and return its content:

```
var HL = require("highland");
var fs = require("fs");

var readFile = HL.wrapCallback(fs.readFile);
var filenames = HL(['file1.txt', 'file2.txt', 'file3.txt']);

filenames
    .map(readFile)
    .parallel(10) //reads up to 10 times at a time
    .each(function(x) {
        console.log("---");
        console.log(x.toString());
        console.log("---");
    });
```

Now, on the preceding code, it's important to note that up to the `parallel` method call, the stream has not been yet been consumed, which means you can still add more transformations before the each method call, but the latter starts consuming the stream, thus pulling values one at the time and adding new transformations after it would not be possible. In fact, the only method that can be called after each is done.

A Word about Backpressure

This term was mentioned earlier a few times, and a small explanation was added next to it, but the truth is, backpressure is quite a relevant term when it comes to stream-based flows, because whether your library implements a strategy for it or not will affect the use-cases supported.

To elaborate, backpressure is the ability of your library to cope with a fast producer, meaning when, for some reason, the consumer of the stream is slower in processing the chunks than the stream itself takes to produce them.

There are basically two ways to handle this scenario: either you accept the loss of data and just take what you can, or you can't afford losing data, so you buffer it somehow. For each approach, there are different strategies, as mentioned here.

Accepting the Loss of Data

The following are three different strategies that can be used to handle a chatty producer when data loss is accepted.

Debouncing the Stream

This technique consists of creating a new stream from the original, but the new one will only emit data after a given timespan has passed without the original stream emitting an event. Basically the debounce operation will filter out events emitted by the source stream that are quickly followed by another event.

Sampling Streams

This one is pretty straightforward: Given a set timespan, it will emit a new event with the latest event emitted by the source stream. Of course, any event emitted in between two sampling events will be ignored.

Pausing the Stream

This method simply consists of pausing the source stream for a given period of time and then resuming it. This will drop everything emitted by the source stream during the pause interval.

When Losing Is Not an Option

The following three strategies deal with the use case when your data are too precious and you cannot afford to lose them due to an over-verbose producer.

Buffering

There are a couple of ways you can buffer the events from the original stream if you need to; for instance, you can set up a max number of events to buffer before pushing them all together down the line. Or you can set an amount of time to put data into the buffer for, and then when the time is up, simply push all those values down the line again.

Buffered Pause

Similar to the previous pause technique, but instead of dropping everything emitted by the source stream during the pause time, it will buffer it. Once you resume, the buffered events will be triggered one by one, thus allowing your code to operate as if nothing happened.

Controlled Streams

Finally, this technique consists of turning the natural behavior of streams, which is a push-based behavior (meaning the producer pushes the events to the consumer), into a pull-based one, having the consumers pull as many events as needed on a given time interval, thus completely controlling the flow of data from the consumer's point of view.

In Conclusion

I could keep on adding more code samples for all the libraries reviewed, but the truth is, this chapter is meant to give you an example of how things are being currently done in the world of functional RP (FRP) libraries for Node.js.

It is also meant to provide you with inspiration for the Chapter 7, when I'll start filling in the code of the FRP library developed in this book.

Table 6-1 summarizes the characteristics of the libraries covered in this chapter.

■ **Note** All three libraries covered in this chapter are great and have almost no down side to using them. But for the sake of comparison, I'll try to list the less-than-ideal features as "Cons".

Table 6-1. *Pros and Cons for All Three Libraries Discussed in This Chapter*

Library / Module	Pros	Cons
RxJS	• Amazingly well documented • Great compatibility • Very mature API with great helper methods • Shares the same API with other Rx* products, helping transition from other technologies • Used by "big" companies, like Netflix, Microsoft, Github and others • It implements back-pressure.	• Not exactly meant for Node.js, you need to install one extra module to be able to use it. • Less control over adding new features thanks to the big group behind it. • Feels like it was built with C# or Java in mind, so there is a bit of object nesting on the API (i.e., RX.Obsevable.case)
Bacon.js	• Great API with lots of helper methods • Simpler API, built with JavaScript in mind • Works natively on Node.js • Nice amount of examples and tutorials available right from their main site	• It doesn't implement back-pressure.
Highland.js	• Implements back-pressure • Small footprint • It's meant to work with Node.js. • It was implemented on top of Node streams.	• Less documentation available • Less helper methods available

Summary

By now you should have a pretty good understanding of the important aspects that every functional reactive library should have. You should also have a pretty decent amount of reference work done by others in this area.

The only thing left for me to do now is to show you a similar approach that will be inspired by what has been covered so far in this book, and that should give you the final insight into how one of these libraries works; ideally, by doing so it will also provide further insight into how reactive programming works.

So, let's move on to the next chapter and write a fresh new FRP library for Node.js, shall we?

CHAPTER 7

■ ■ ■

Writing Your Own FRP Library

You've finally reached the chapter where everything gets put into practice, or almost everything, mind you. In this chapter, I'm going to take into account everything covered so far, that means: functional programming, reactive programming, Node.js (obviously!) and the examples provided by the libraries that already exist and with that, I'm going to write the first version of a new FRP library for Node.

The point of this chapter is not to improve over the currently published modules that I just went over. Instead, it's purpose is to provide an inside view of what it would be like to create one of those libraries. In other words, knowing how something works, will help you understand the concepts involved, even if the implementation provided here is not exactly that of the already reviewed libraries (and it's not) you'll be able to see one possible way to solve the implementation-related issues.

By the end of this chapter, you'll have a pretty good idea on how to implement a Functional Reactive library and how to publish it on Node's npm public registry.

First things first, let's discuss the type of library I'm going to be writing. As I stated before, this library will obviously be inspired by the three discussed in the previous chapter (that is: RxJS, Bacon.js and Highland.js).

Because the implementation itself could take several months, let alone the actual review of the code, this new library will only have the bare minimum functionality required to execute a set of common reactive actions, such as queuing up transformations, merging streams and minor timing functions, like debouncing a stream.

That being said, it should provide enough of a framework for you to start playing with and extend if needed to create your own version of the library that would suit your very specific needs.

I'm going to describe the internal architecture of the library, which I've so aptly named R-CheeseJS (I know right?). You'll see that I'm actually following a very simple and easy-to-extend architecture here, again, allowing you to easily add more functionality to it if so you desired. You'll be able to get the code for R-Cheese with the book, or from GitHub (at https://github.com/deleteman/r-cheese).

The code of R-Cheese is grouped into two files, one for the main library, which will have very few public methods and another one for the utility functions, which will be the main attraction, and they will contain the functionality that you'll be mostly using.

The Big Cheese

The main library, which is the one you'll always have to use, was designed to work on top of a Node.js stream, this simplifies things, because I didn't have the need to simulate the way a stream would work (in regards of time-based events, data being transferred, and so on), Node already did it for me, so what this library does, is it provides a simpler interface to interact with a Node stream and also, it provides simple ways to transform the data that flows through it.

© Fernando Doglio 2016
F. Doglio, *Reactive Programming with Node.js*, DOI 10.1007/978-1-4842-2152-5_7

The methods you'll want to pay attention to from a user point of view are:

- **fromStream**: This method will create a Cheese stream from a regular Node.js stream (every 'data' event on this stream will write to the internal cheese stream).

- **fromArray**: Again, this one will create a new Cheese stream from a good old Array object. Array items will be emitted every 100 milliseconds (default value) or given a delay period provided as a second, optional, parameter.

- **fromFn**: The last of the fromXXX methods, this one will create a new Cheese stream from the emitted values of a function. It basically works like the previous one, but it gives you more control over what is emitted and when it is emitted. This method receives a second, optional parameter to set the delay for emitting the values, just like above (but the default value is 0 milliseconds, since you can define the timing from within the function as well. The function passed as emitter will receive a single function as parameter, which will have to be called every time a new value needs to be emitted.

- **merge**: This method will merge the current internal stream with any other stream passed as parameter. The order of the resulting data chunks is only determined by the timing of the different data events.

- **then**: This method will simply act as syntactic sugar, allowing you to chain transformations over the data chunks being transferred through the stream. It only receives a single function per call.

- **onError**: Just like the above method, but it sets up a special chain of transformations that will take place only when one of the transformation emits an error (either by throwing an exception or by passing an error parameter to its callback).

- **each**: Finally, this should be the last method to be called on every chain of transformations. It starts the execution of the stream up to the point when this method is called and receives a final function that will be called at the end of the transformation chain with the final resulting value.

Let's now look at a few examples of the above methods, and then I'll show you the code for them. The first one shows you how to interact with existing Node.js streams using the fromStream method:

```
var Cheese  = require("./cheese").Cheese;
var fs = require("fs");

var ch = new Cheese();
var chStream = ch.fromStream(fs.createReadStream('./test-cheese1.js'));

chStream
    .each(function(content) {
        console.log(content.toString());
    });
```

As you can see, the above example is quite simple, but it shows both the fromStream method, and the mandatory usage of the each method, without it, the reading of the file would've never started. You can easily add some transformations to it by using the then method before calling each, like so:

```
//rewriting the final lines of the previous example
chStream
    .then(function(chunk) {
        return chunk.toString().toUpperCase();
    })
    .each(function(content) {
        console.log(content.toString());
    });
```

By default you can pass any function to the then method, and it will check whether it receives one parameter (assuming it's a synchronous function) or two (assuming it's an asynchronous function) and it will operate accordingly.

Let's now look at one final example, with and without error handling:

```
var Cheese = require("r-cheese").Cheese;
var fs = require("fs");

var flatMap = require("r-cheese").Utils.flatMap;
var ch = new Cheese();

var filenames = ['./test-cheese1.js', './test-cheese23.js'];
ch.fromArray(filenames)
.then(flatMap(function(name) {
    return fs.createReadStream(name.toString());
}))
.each(function(content) {
    console.log(content.toString());
});
```

Ignoring for now the use of the flatMap function (I'll get into it in a second), the above code simply takes a list of filepaths, and transforms it into the actual file content of each element. It also ends up printing the content out. Now if one of those filepaths were to have a typo, you'll end up with an unhandled exception printed on screen, because the fs.createReadStream line would generate an error event and you have nothing to handled that event. In fact, because of the way Node.js handles the error events and because you're not listening for it, your script will be terminated (I mentioned this in a previous chapter, remember?)

You can easily fix that by adding error handling using the onError method, like so:

```
ch.fromArray(filenames)
.then(flatMap(function(name) {
    return fs.createReadStream(name.toString())
}))
.onError(function(e) {
    console.trace(e);
})
.each(function(cnt) {
    console.log(cnt.toString());
});
```

And with that, you're now safely handling the error event, your script will not be prematurely terminated and you'll have full control over what to do with that error.

■ **Note** The chunks of data that generate an error will not be processed by any of the following transformations, but the following chunks will go through the entire chain as they should (provided they don't also generate an error as well).

Let's now look at the code for the main library, shall we?

```
var Streams = require("stream");
var inherits = require("util").inherits;

var Transform = Streams.Transform;

function OutputStream() {
    Transform.call(this);
}

inherits(OutputStream, Transform);

OutputStream.prototype._transform = function(chunk, encoding, callback) {
    callback(null, chunk);
}

var DEFAULT_ARRAY_DELAY = 100; //ms
var DEFAULT_FN_DELAY = 0; //ms
```

The preceding lines are simply to define our internal stream, and a couple of default values used bellow.

```
function Cheese(stream, transformations) {
    this._stream = stream || null;
    this._stream_ended = false;
    this._outputStream = new OutputStream();
    if(this._stream !== null) {
        this.fromStream(stream)
    }
    this._transformations = transformations || [];
    this._error_transformations = [];
    this._source_name = null;
    this._source_interval = null;
    this._source_interval_delay = null;
    this._source_interval_origin = null;
}

Cheese.prototype.fromStream = function(stream) {
    var self = this;
    this._stream = stream;
    this._source_name = 'stream';
```

```
        this._stream.on('data', function(d) {
            self._writeToOutput(d);
        });
        return this;
};

Cheese.prototype.fromFn = function(fn, delay) {
    if(typeof delay == 'undefined') {
        delay = DEFAULT_FN_DELAY;
    }

    this._source_name = 'fn';
    this._source_interval_delay = delay;
    this._source_interval_origin = fn;

    return this;
};

Cheese.prototype.fromArray = function(arr, delay) {
    if(typeof delay == 'undefined') {
        delay = DEFAULT_ARRAY_DELAY;
    }

    this._source_name = 'array';
    this._source_interval_delay = delay;
    this._source_interval_origin = arr;

    return this;
};
```

The previous three methods setup the gathering of events, depending on the source (array, function or stream), note that these methods only setup the right values on the right variables, only when the each method is called, the actual intervals will be started (see below).

```
Cheese.prototype._writeToOutput = function(val) {
    if(!this._stream_ended) {
        if(val !== null) {
            val = val.toString();
        }
        this._outputStream.write(val);
    }
}
```

The previous method centralizes the writes on the internal stream, remember that the entire library is basically handling the flow of data and transforming it to eventually writing it into an internal stream, this method is the one that takes care of that last bit.

Once the library starts pulling data from the set source, every chunk goes through the chain of transformations set using the then methods, the following methods take care of executing those transformations, applying them to the data and passing on the result to the next one on the list. They are different variations of the same thing, depending on the type of helper transformation function they're executing, different parameters (or even behaviors) are needed. There is a default one called _execute_ normal that will be called for simple functions (i.e custom transformation functions instead of the ones

provided by the library) . If you're extending this library and adding new transformations, you can rely on
_execute_normal or add new specific handlers here. Now in no particular order, here are the methods:

```
Cheese.prototype._execute_filter = function(idx, value, handler, transforms) {
    var self = this;

    transforms[idx](value, function(err, resp) {
        if(!err && !!resp === true) {
            if(transforms.length > idx + 1) {
                self._execute(++idx, value, handler, transforms);
            } else {
                handler(value);
            }
        }
    });
};

Cheese.prototype._execute_normal = function(idx, value, handler, transforms) {
    var self = this;

    if(transforms.length == 0) {
        return handler(value);
    }
    var fn = transforms[idx];

    if(fn.length == 2) {
        //check the number of arguments the function receives
        fn(value, function(err, resp ) {
            if(err) {
                return self._execute(0, err, handler, self._error_transformations);
            }
            if(transforms.length > idx + 1) {
                self._execute(++idx, resp, handler, transforms);
            } else {
                handler(resp);
            }
        });
    } else {
        try {
            var resp = fn(value);
            if(transforms.length > idx + 1) {
                self._execute(++idx, resp, handler, transforms);
            } else {
                if(handler) {
                    handler(resp);
                }
            }
        } catch (err ) {
            self._execute(0, err, handler, self._error_transformations);
        }
    }
};
```

The previous function allows for a synchronous or an asynchronous custom transformation to be executed and it's errors handled properly. To clarity, if the custom transformation only receives one parameter (you can find that out by querying the length property of the function by the way) I'm assuming this function is synchronous, because it only receives the value to transform, but if it receives two, then I'm assuming the second one is the callback and it's an asynchronous function (it makes no sense to define custom transformations with more than two parameters, because the library would not know what to pass on the extra ones).

Error handling is done by either catching the exceptions for synchronous functions or checking the error on the callback for the asynchronous version and then passing in that to the chain of error transformations.

```
Cheese.prototype._execute_reduce = function(idx, value, handler, transforms) {
    var self = this;
    transforms[idx](this._outputStream, value, function(resp) {
        if(transforms.length > idx + 1) {
            self._execute(++idx, resp, handler, transforms);
        } else {
            handler(resp);
        }
    });

};
```

The reduce helper function (which I'll show further down the chapter) works by applying the same transformation to all values of the stream until it ends, and then emitting the final value. In order to know when the stream ends, the function needs the actual stream object, which is why the above method is passing it as the first parameter to the function.

The split function is a very simple synchronous one, so the following method takes care of executing it calling the next step on the chain.

```
Cheese.prototype._execute_split = function(idx, value, handler, transforms) {
    var self = this;
    var parts = transforms[idx](value);
    if(transforms.length > idx + 1) {
        self._execute(++idx, parts, handler, transforms);
    } else {
        handler(parts);
    }
};
```

```
Cheese.prototype._execute_flatmap = function(idx, value, handler, transforms) {
    var self = this;
    transforms[idx](value, this._error_transformations, function(err, resp) {
        if(err) {
            return self._execute(0, err, handler, self._error_transformations);
        }
        if(transforms.length > idx + 1) {
            self._execute(++idx, resp, handler, transforms);
        } else {
            handler(resp);
        }
    });

};
```

The flatMap transformation creates a new stream from the results of the function it receives, so in order to keep the same error chain on the new stream, I'm passing it to the flatMap function, and as you'll see in a bit, that function will take the error handling chain and add it to the new stream. This way if something fails after the flatMap is executed, the errors will still be correctly handled,

For the take helper functions (take, takeUntil and takeWhile) I needed a way to signal the end of the internal stream from within the helper function, which is why I needed access to the stream and which is why I'm passing it as parameter in the following method.

```
Cheese.prototype._execute_take_transform = function(idx, value, handler, transforms) {
    var self = this;
    transforms[idx](this._outputStream, value, function(err, resp) {
        if(err) {
            return self._execute(0, err, handler, self._error_transformations);
        }
        if(transforms.length > idx + 1) {
            self._execute(++idx, resp, handler, transforms);
        } else {
            handler(resp);
        }
    });

};


Cheese.prototype._execute_debounce_throttle = function(idx, value, handler, transforms) {
    var self = this;
    transforms[idx](this, value, idx, handler, transforms, function(newStream) {
        if(transforms.length > idx + 1) {
            self._execute(++idx, value, handler, transforms);
        } else {
            handler(value);
        }
    });
};
```

Finally, the last of this batch of methods takes care of executing the debounce and throttle helper functions, those are very special, because they have to deal with modifying the timing of the events, essentially modifying the original source of data. This is why I'm passing in the this object as the first parameter, by having access to the entire Cheese object, the helper function can overwrite the way data is emitted (you'll see more details about it when I show you that code further down this chapter).

```
Cheese.prototype._execute = function(idx, value, handler, transforms) {

    var fnType = transforms[idx] ? transforms[idx].__fn_type : null;
    var execs = {
        'filter': this._execute_filter.bind(this),
        'reduce': this._execute_reduce.bind(this),
        'split': this._execute_split.bind(this),
        'take': this._execute_take_transform.bind(this), //takes care of all 3 types of take
        'debounce': this._execute_debounce_throttle.bind(this),
        'throttle': this._execute_debounce_throttle.bind(this),
        'flatMap': this._execute_flatmap.bind(this)
    };
```

```
    if(execs[fnType]) {
        execs[fnType](idx, value, handler, transforms);
    } else {
        this._execute_normal(idx, value, handler, transforms);
    }
};
```

The preceding method takes care of picking the right helper method to execute the helper function at the current position of the transformation chain. Basically, every helper function provided by the library (as you'll soon see) has a __fn_type attribute, which identifies the type of helper function it is (i.e "map" for the map function, "take" for all the different take functions, etc), so using that attribute, the _execute method can choose the right helper to use, or default to one that should be able to handle generic transformation functions.

The following method handles the merging of a new stream into the current one, simply by subscribing to the data event and writing each chunk to the internal stream (which is the common stream where all data is written).

```
Cheese.prototype.merge = function(newStream) {
    var self = this;
    newStream.on('data', function(d) {
        self._writeToOutput(d);
    });

    return this;
}

Cheese.prototype.each = function(handler) {
    var self = this;
    var index = 0;
    //we need to create a new list of transformations up to this point
    //that way when the 'data' event is triggered, only the current list of transformations
    //will be executed for this handler
    var transforms = this._transformations.map(function(t) {
        if(t.newInstance) {
            return t.newInstance();
        }
        return t;
    });

    //start the chain of transformations
    this._outputStream.on('data', function(d) {
        self._execute(index, d, handler, transforms);
    });

    this._outputStream.on('finish', function() {
        self._endSource();
    });

    if(this._source_name == 'fn' && !this._source_interval) {
        self._source_interval = setInterval(function() {
            self._source_interval_origin(function(value) {
```

```
                if(value === null) {
                    return self._endSource();
                }
                self._writeToOutput(value);
            })
        }, self._source_interval_delay);
    }
    if(this._source_name == 'array' && !this._source_interval) {
        this._source_interval = setInterval(function() {
            if(self._source_interval_origin.length > 0) {
                self._writeToOutput(self._source_interval_origin.shift());
            } else {
                self._endSource();
            }
        }, this._source_interval_delay);
    }
};
```

The previous method has one simple responsibility from the developer standpoint, but as you can appreciate, internally, it takes care of several tasks:

- It creates a copy of the list of transformations up to the point when it is called. This way, you can call it in different parts of the stream in order to react partially while the data is being transformed (I showed a similar example when discussing the Bacon.js library in the previous chapter).

- It also takes care of starting the chain of transformations, up to this point you were setting up transformations but until this method is called, no data is flowing through the chain.

- It makes sure to call the _endSource method once the stream is over (this is especially helpful if you are dealing with a function as a source of data).

- Finally, it creates the intervals required to pull information from non stream sources, like functions and arrays.

Also, please note how the interval set for the array source makes a point of calling _endSource once there are no more items to emit, while the interval set for a function source, doesn't, that means the function will have to write a null value to notify it has no more data to transmit.

The following three methods are short and simple to understand, but for the sake of completeness I'll go over them real quick:

- _endSource: This method takes care of ending the source of data in the proper way, depending on what it is. For interval-related sources, it will clear the interval, for streams, it will end the stream. This method would need to be extended if further type of data sources were to be added.

- then: Simple method, it adds transformations to the list and returns the object itself, to keep chaining method calls.

- onError: This method sets the error handling chain and adds functions to it. And if the data source is a stream, it also subscribes itself to the error event, that way it makes sure the app is not killed by Node.js as it would otherwise.

```
Cheese.prototype._endSource = function() {
    this._stream_ended = true;
    switch(this._source_name) {
        case 'stream':
            this._stream.end();
            break;
        case 'array':
        case 'fn':
            this._outputStream.end();
            clearInterval(this._source_interval);
            break;
    }
};

Cheese.prototype.then = function(fn) {
    this._transformations.push(fn);
    return this;
};

Cheese.prototype.onError = function(fn) {
    var self = this;
    //The first time we set an error handler if we're dealing with a fromStream case, we
    make sure that
    //the error event is taken care of
    if(this._error_transformations.length == 0 && this._source_name == 'stream') {
        this._stream.on('error', function(err) {
            self._execute(0, err, null, self._error_transformations);
        });
    }
    this._error_transformations.push(fn);
    return this;
};
module.exports = Cheese;
```

This concludes the analysis of the main library, let me know show you the code for the helper functions, which should also provide some interesting read.

The Little Cheese

This first version of R-Cheese provides a total of nine transformations and are exported as individual functions to simplify the task of adding more, simply add the new function to the utils.js file and export it.

Even though the exported transformations are quite different from each other, the structure of the functions that define them is always the same, they basically use the following template:

```
function transformation([params]) {
    var _fn = function([params]) {
        //your code here
    };
    _fn.__fn_type = '[FUNCTION TYPE IDENTIFIER]';
```

```
    _fn.newInstance = function() {
        //your code here
    };

    return _fn;
}
```

Every transformation function is actually a wrapper for the actual function that does the work. Thanks to the fact that functions in JavaScript are also objects, I can add some properties to it, mainly __fn_type which is a string identifying the type of transformation (this is used by the _execute method on the main library's code as you already saw) and the newInstance method, which basically should return a new instance of the transformation (you can find this method being used on the main library's each method).

So let me now go over each transformation built into the code, some of them have already been covered in past chapters and some of them might be new to you, so hopefully, with the explanation and the code you should have no problem understanding them.

Map, Filter, and Reduce

These three are the most common ones out there, and I've covered them in past chapters as well, so there is not a lot to say about them that I haven't already said. So instead, let me just show you the implementation for them:

```
function map(fn) {
    var _fn = function(value, done){
        fn(value, done); //this version of the map function is asynchronous, so it requires
        a callback
    };
    _fn.__fn_type = 'map';
    _fn.newInstance = function() {
        return map(fn);
    };
    return _fn;
}

function filter(fn) {
    var _fn = function(value, done) {
        fn(value, done);
    };
    _fn.__fn_type = 'filter';
    _fn.newInstance = function() {
        return filter(fn);
    };
    return _fn;
}
function reduce(init, fn) {
    var accu = init;
    var listenerSet = false;

    var _fn = function(stream, value, done) {
        accu = fn(accu , value);
        if(!listenerSet) {
```

```
                stream.on('end', function() {
                    done(accu );
                });
                listenerSet = true;
            }
        };
        _fn.__fn_type = 'reduce';
        _fn.newInstance = function() {
            return reduce(init, fn);
        };
        return _fn;
}
```

As you can see, all three functions follow the template I showed before. The first one, the map function is nothing much really, it is the simplest one in the bunch, and it only acts as syntactic sugar since all it does, is execute the function received as parameter. Because of the _execute_normal method on the main library, doing a map or simply passing an anonymous function to the then method does the same thing.

The filter function is quite simple as well, in-fact, its code is almost exactly the same as the map one, with the only difference of a different function type identifier, which in turn, tells the main library how to interpret the output of this function and what to do with it.

Finally, the reduce function (also known can scan in other libraries), will accumulate the chunks in the manner specified by the function received, and once the stream ends, it will emit the accumulated result. As you can see, that is the reason why this function requires the stream to be passed as parameter, it needs to subscribe to the end event of the internal stream.

Take and Take Some More

There are three variants of the take function here, the simple one will accept a fixed amount of chunks from the stream and then it will end it, this is the take function. The second one, the takeUntil function, will accept chunks from the source of data until the condition of the function passed as parameter is met (basically, when the function returns true). And finally, takeWhile, which is quite similar to takeUntil, but the condition is the opposite, it will accept chunks *while* the condition is met, afterwards, the data will not flow past this point.

Let's first take a look at their code:

```
function take(number) {
    var counter = 0;
    var max = number;

    var _fn = function(stream, value, done) {
        counter++;
        if(counter == max) {
            stream.end();
        }
        return done(null, value);
    };

    _fn.__fn_type = 'take';
    _fn.newInstance = function() {
        return take(number);
    };
    return _fn;
}
```

```javascript
function takeUntil(condition) {

    var _fn = function(stream, value, done) {
        if(condition.length === 1) {
            if(condition(value)) {
                return stream.end();
            }
            return done(null, value);
        } else {
            condition(value, function(err, resp) {
                if(!!resp === true) {
                    return stream.end();
                }
                return done(err, value);
            });
        }

    };

    _fn.__fn_type = 'take';
    _fn.newInstance = function() {
        return takeUntil(condition);
    };
    return _fn;
}

function takeWhile(condition) {

    var _fn = function(stream, value, done) {
        if(condition.length === 1) {
            if(!condition(value)) {
                return stream.end();
            }
            return done(null, value);
        } else {
            condition(value, function(err, resp) {
                if(!!resp === false) {
                    return stream.end();
                }
                return done(err, value);
            });
        }

    };

    _fn.__fn_type = 'take';
    _fn.newInstance = function() {
        return takeWhile(condition);
    };
    return _fn;
}
```

Their code is very similar to each other, and they even share the same function type identifier, because the main library can handle the three of them in the same manner. Finally, both takeUntil and takeWhile accept both an asynchronous and a synchronous function as the condition for deciding when to stop. Figure 7-1 gives you an example of how all three variations behave.

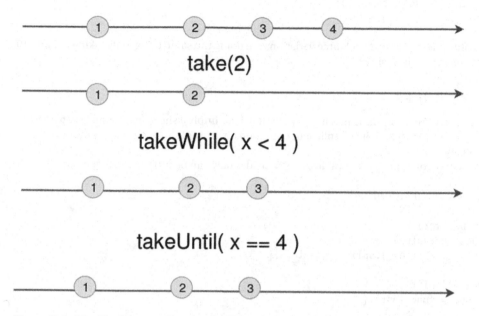

Figure 7-1. *Marble diagram showing the differences between all three take methods*

Let's quickly check out a code sample for these methods:

```
var cheese = require("./cheese").Cheese;
var _ = require("lodash");

var take = require("./cheese").Utils.take;
var takeUntil = require("./cheese").Utils.takeUntil;
var takeWhile = require("./cheese").Utils.takeWhile;
var ch = new cheese();
var ch1 = new cheese();
var ch2 = new cheese();

ch.fromArray(_.range(100)).then(take(10)).each(function(v) {
    console.log("Ch: ", v.toString());
});

ch1.fromArray(_.range(100)).then(takeWhile(function(v) {
    //the value needs to be coerced into an integer, because all data that flows through the
    stream is casted into a String.
    return +v < 11;
}))
.each(function(v) {
    console.log("Ch1: ", v.toString());
});
```

```
ch2.fromArray(_.range(100)).then(takeUntil(function(v) {
    return +v > 10;
}))
.each(function(v) {
    console.log("Ch2: ", v.toString());
})
```

As you've probably guessed already, all three variations are doing the same thing, only taking the first 10 elements of the stream and then closing it.

Splitting Your Chunks

This one is pretty straightforward, nothing much to say about it, it is simply a shortcut to doing a map and then a string split inside it. By default it will split your strings on an array of single characters unless you pass it a separator string.

The result of this function is an array of values, which incidentally can be turned into a new stream using flatMap.

Here is the code for this transformation:

```
function split(separator) {
    var _fn = function(value) {
        return value.toString().split(separator || "");
    }
    _fn.__fn_type = 'split';
    _fn.newInstance = function() {
        return _fn;
    }
    return _fn;
}
```

Now, let's check out this example regarding the usage of split and flatMap together:

```
var cheese = require("./cheese").Cheese;

var flatMap = require("./cheese").Utils.flatMap;
var split = require("./cheese").Utils.split;

var ch = new cheese();

var words = ["test", "goodbye"];

ch.fromArray(words)
.then(split())
.then(flatMap(function(arr) {
    return arr
}))
.onError(function(e) {
    console.trace(e)
})
.each(function(cnt) {
    console.log("Ch: ", cnt.toString());
});
```

The output of the above code, might not be exactly what you think, check it Figure 7-2 for a screenshot:

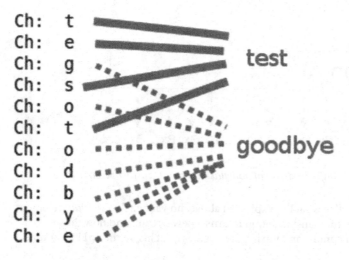

Figure 7-2. *Mixed output of the above code*

Because the `flatMap` function is actually creating two different streams, one from each array returned by `split`, you end-up with two source streams working in parallel, as if you had just merged them into one, that is the reason why some of those letters are mixed and it's not just one word after the other.

FlatMap and the Plot Thickens

This one is the first of the three most complex transformations provided in this code, the next two deal with timing issues, but that's not the case here.

I've been using this transformation on several examples in this chapter without going into much details, so you might've already picked up on what it is that this function is supposed to do, or maybe you're as baffled by it as I was the first 10 times I read about, so let me try to explain it as simply as possible.

The `flatMap` function has the ability to create a new stream from the returned value of the function it receives. Now that returned value should be something that the library knows how to use as a source of data for a stream, that is:

- Another stream (check out example where `flatMap` returns the resulting stream of executing `fs.createReadStream`).

- An array (checkout the example shown before).

- A function, which of course would have to comply with the required behavior expected by `fromFn`.

If used right, this transformation can provide a great deal of flexibility to your streams. Checkout Figure 7-3 to see how it works.

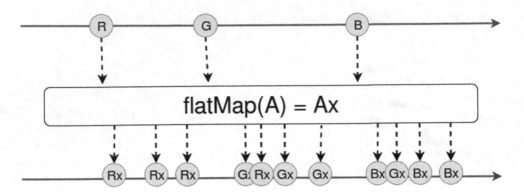

Figure 7-3. *A marble diagram showing a simplified version of how flatMap can transform a stream*

Figure 7-3 takes care of putting graphically, what I've explained above, how for each *observable* element returned by the function passed to flatMap, the transformation returns a new stream, and how those resulting streams are actually all working in parallel and mixing their values (just like in the split example from before).

The code for this transformation is the as follows (this function also provides the developer with the ability to have both a synchronous and an asynchronous function as parameter of flatMap):

```
function flatMap(fn) {
    var _fn;
    var observable;
    var newStream = null;

    function setEachEvent(stream, observable, error_transforms, done) {
        if(Array.isArray(observable)) {
            stream.fromArray(observable)
        } else if(typeof observable === 'function') {
            stream.fromFn(observable);
        } else if(observable instanceof _streams) {
            stream.fromStream(observable);
        }
        error_transforms.forEach(function(et) {
            stream.onError(et);
        })

        //for each item emitted by newStream
        //insert it into the original stream
        //**at the right place**
        stream.each(function(v) {
            done(null, v);
        });
    }
```

```
    if(fn.length == 1) {
        _fn = function(value, error_transforms, done) {
            newStream = new Cheese();
            try {
                observable = fn(value);
            } catch (e) {
                return done(e);
            }
            setEachEvent(newStream, observable, error_transforms, done);
        };
    } else {
        _fn = function(value, error_transforms, done) {
            newStream = new Cheese();
            fn(value, function(err, observable) {
                if(err) {
                    return done(err);
                }
                setEachEvent(newStream, observable, error_transforms, done);
            });
        };
    }
    _fn.__fn_type = 'flatMap';
    _fn.newInstance = function() {
        return flatMap(fn);
    }
    return _fn;
}
```

Quite literally, the transformation is creating a new stream from the resulting output of the passed function. The done callback is the link back to the original chain of transformations and the _fn function is also receiving the chain of error transformations to make sure the new stream is aware of it (that way if an error occurs on the new stream, the same chain of error transformations is applied in a transparent way for the developer).

Dealing With Time

The last two transformations deal with the timing of events on the stream, because sometimes dealing with every single chunk of data received is not what the developer needs, in fact, some of those events might be repeated, especially if they're user generated events (not applicable for the back-end but click events on the front-end are a very common example here).

That is why two transformations are provided to deal with such cases (although more exist and can easily be added if required): debounce and throttle. And although they might seem to be doing the same thing at first glance, their behavior is not exactly the same and the results might be unpredictable if one is used when the other should've been.

Let's start with debounce first, the idea behind this one, is that given a stream of events, you want to remove the ones that are too close together for whatever reason, so you can set a delay time and tell the transformation to debounce the events using that delay. Let's see Figure 7-4 first and then I'll explain more:

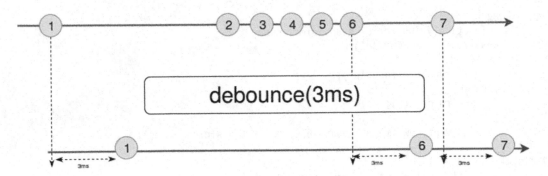

Figure 7-4. *Marble diagram for the debounce function*

So, again, given a stream of events, debouncing them based on a time delay, means emitting only the last event received after there have been no other events for the last [delay] period of time. In the diagram of Figure 7-4, the input is debounced by 3 milliseconds, which means that after a value is received, if no other value is received within those 3 milliseconds then it will be emitted otherwise it will be ignored. That is why values 2,3,4 and 5 are ignored by 6 is emitted.

Now, on the other hand, throttling a stream is similar, yet, different. For this one, what it means is that it will emit one event every time the delay is up, and if several events happened in the middle, only the last one will be emitted, and the rest will be ignored. Figure 7-5 shows the diagram for throttle:

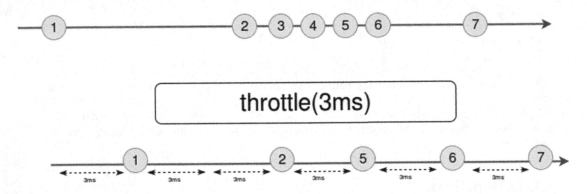

Figure 7-5. *Marble diagram for the throttle transformation*

Using the same source stream and the same time delay, you can see how the result is different from the previous one, in this case, the values 2 and 5 are also emitted, because they were the last ones received during the 3 millisecond intervals.

Here are two code examples that show how you can use throttle and debounce in your code (they're made up example with no real world application but you'll get to that in future chapters, don't worry):

```
var cheese = require("r-cheese").Cheese;

var ch = new cheese();
var debounce = require("r-cheese").Utils.debounce;
```

```
var source = [
 //v is the value to emit, d is the delay to wait before emitting it.
    {v: "hola", d: 10},
    {v: "adios", d: 1},
    {v: "goodbye", d: 1},
    {v: "hello", d: 5}];

var lastTimestamp = 0;
var index = 0;
ch.fromFn(function(push) {

    if(Date.now() - lastTimestamp > source[index].d) {
        console.log("Pushing value: ", source[index].v)
        push(source[index].v)
        lastTimestamp = Date.now();
        index++;
    }
    if(index == source.length) {
        push(null);
    }

}).then(debounce(5)).each(function(n) {
    console.log("::Received value: ", n.toString());
});
```

The above example for the debounce function will emit a series of values in different moments of time, with a debounce set of 5 milliseconds, the output is shown on Figure 7-6:

Pushing value: hola
::Received value: hola
Pushing value: adios   •••••••• Ignored
Pushing value: goodbye ••••••
Pushing value: hello
::Received value: hello

Figure 7-6. Output of debounce example

As for the throttle function, here's the example:

```
var cheese = require("r-cheese").Cheese;

var ch = new cheese();
var throttle = require("r-cheese").Utils.throttle;

var source = [
    {v: "hola", d: 1},
    {v: "adios", d: 3000},
    {v: "goodbye", d: 1000},
    {v: "hello", d: 2000},
    {v: null, d: 1000}];
```

119

```
var lastTimestamp = 0;
var index = 0;
ch.fromFn(function(push) {
    if(Date.now() - lastTimestamp > source[index].d) {
        console.log("Pushing value: ", source[index].v)
        push(source[index].v)
        lastTimestamp = Date.now();
        index++;
    }
}).then(throttle(2500)).each(function(n) {
    console.log("::Received value: ", n.toString());
});
```

The example above has the same mechanics of the debounce example, only this time, the intervals are higher to correctly demonstrate the effect of throttle. On the example, I'm throttling the data on intervals of 2.5 seconds, so, as expected, the output is shown on Figure 7-7:

Pushing value: hola ■■■■■■■■■■■■■■■■■■■ 0 secs
::Received value: hola ━━━━━━━━ 2.5 secs
Pushing value: adios ■■■■■■■■■■■■■■■■■■■ 3 secs
Pushing value: goodbye ■■■■■■■■■■■■■■■■■ 4 secs
::Received value: goodbye ━━━━━━━ 5 secs
Pushing value: hello ■■■■■■■■■■■■■■■■■■ 6 secs
Pushing value: null■■■■■■■■■■■■■■■■■■■ 7 secs

Figure 7-7. *Output of the throttle example*

The moments when the data is written into the stream are marked with the dotted lines, and as you can see, the moments from the interval of the throttle are marked with a continuous line and as desired, only two values make it through to the end, the rest are ignored.

Now that you've seen how they're both used, let me show you their implementation:

```
function debounce(delay) {

    var lastTimestamp = null;
    var debounced = false;
    var listeners = [];

    var _fn = function(cheese, value, index, handler, transforms, done) {
        var now = null;

        if(debounced) {
            return done(cheese._outputStream);
        }
        /*
        Remove all active listeners on outgoing stream
        */
```

```
        listeners = cheese._outputStream.listeners('data');
        listeners.map(function(fn) {
            cheese._outputStream.removeListener('data', fn);
        });
        /*
        Overwrite the main listener for the 'data' event on the outgoing stream.
        This way we can control when to actually start the transformations and when to
        ignore the data
        */
        cheese._outputStream.on('data', function(v) {
            now = Date.now();
            if(!lastTimestamp) {
                lastTimestamp = Date.now();
            }
            if(now - lastTimestamp > delay) {
                cheese._execute(index, v, handler, transforms);
            }
            lastTimestamp = now;
        });

        debounced = true;

        return done(cheese._outputStream);
    };
    _fn.__fn_type = 'debounce';
    _fn.newInstance = function() {
        return debounce(delay);
    };
    return _fn;

}


function throttle(delay) {

    var throttled = false;
    var listeners = [];
    var bufferedValue = null;
    var interval = null;

    var _fn = function(cheese, value, index, handler, transforms, done) {
        if(throttled) {
            return done(cheese._outputStream);
        }
        listeners = cheese._outputStream.listeners('data');
        listeners.forEach(function(fn) {
            cheese._outputStream.removeListener('data', fn);
        });
        bufferedValue = value;
        //buffer the last value emitted by  the stream until the moment is right to pass it
        along
```

```
        cheese._outputStream.on('data', function(v) {
            bufferedValue = v;
        });
        if(!interval) { //we start the interval when the first event arrives
                interval = setInterval(function() {
                    if(bufferedValue !== null) {
                        cheese._execute(index, bufferedValue, handler, transforms);
                        bufferedValue = null;
                    }
                }, delay);
        }

        //make sure we clear the active interval when we're done
        cheese._outputStream.on('finish', function() {
            clearInterval(interval);
        })

        throttled = true;
    };
    _fn.__fn_type = 'throttle';
    _fn.newInstance = function() {
        return throttle(delay);
    };
    return _fn;

}
```

Despite having a similar behavior, their implementations are quite different as you can see, debounce needs to pay a lot of attention to timing whilst throttle simply sets an interval and buffers the last value received until the interval is fired. The rest of the logic is quite self explanatory now that you've seen the marble diagrams and the examples there is very little for me to explain.

■ **Caution** The intervals created in Node.js are not super precise in regards of their timing, when you set an interval to execute a function every X milliseconds, it actually will execute it **at least every X milliseconds.** What that means is that Node.js tries it's best to comply with the timing set but the only sure thing is that the function will not be executed before time. When your interval timing is high enough, you won't have a problem, but if you're dealing with very low time limits (like 10 milliseconds or less), you might start running into timing issues.

Summary

Hopefully, this chapter has given you the last bit of insight you needed to fully understand and adopt Functional Reactive Programming on Node.js.

The library described in this chapter is the framework for you to create your own FRP library by adding the extra transformations you need. They will mostly be variations of the existing ones and maybe a few new ones, but you should have everything you need to do it.

Now that you have this library, in the next chapter I'll analyze some examples of FRP in the back-end, both done by other and one specific case solved using R-CheeseJS.

CHAPTER 8

■ ■ ■

A Practical Overview

With the book so far, you've read every bit of theory about functional reactive programming (FRP) I've thrown at you. You also have a working implementation of an FRP library to play with, so you might be wondering: What else is there?

Well, in this chapter I'm going to go over some examples of real-world companies going the reactive way, and I'll try to analyze their reasons and their results. Note that even though these companies will not be using Node.js specifically for this purpose, the reactive paradigm still applies and you'll be able to extrapolate the situation to fit your reality.

Finally, and because I know you want it, I'll throw even more code your way, by creating a somewhat usable application (bearing in mind the limitations imposed by the fact that you'll be reading the code from this book and I don't want to bore you to death) that works on top of the R-Cheese library.

The Case for Netflix

Netflix is probably one of the hottest companies in the world right now, even if it's just because their name is so well known almost anywhere where there is Internet. But something not everyone usually thinks about is that Netflix is a great IT company as well!

Because of the technical challenges that derive from its streaming business, Netflix is constantly forced to push the edge of the technologies it uses. For a few years now, they've been one of the main speakers in favor of Node.js used on the enterprise scene. And recently they've been pushing the Functional Reactive approach, both on the back-end and the front-end. And because they've been so kind as to publish their experience on their tech blog (http://techblog.netflix.com) I can now go over it.

Their Motivation

The initial architecture behind Netflix's back-end was based on a series of RESTful APIs that provided a generic platform on which their multiple client applications could rely. That was the up side to it, the down side, though, was that because it was generic and meant to serve very different clients, each service would only return a portion of the data needed for the client's features.

Those mechanics eventually got out of hand when their users numbers got high enough, because every client would need to make too many requests for a single page, and for every request, you have to add network latency to the time equation (not only affecting page-load times but also affecting internal service communications). In the end, they decided to go with a different approach. Check out Figure 8-1 for a visual representation of that problem.

© Fernando Doglio 2016
F. Doglio, *Reactive Programming with Node.js*, DOI 10.1007/978-1-4842-2152-5_8

Figure 8-1 shows the basic idea behind the classic RESTful API-based architecture. The image represents a single client's requests for one feature. Several pieces of information might be needed for a single page rendering, so several requests are made, which in turn adds network latency for every request. You can see how this can get out of hand.

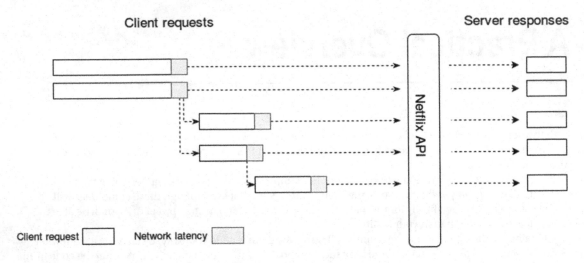

Figure 8-1. *Diagram showing the mechanics of the original Netflix architecture*

Instead, they decided to switch things around and moved the logic needed to create the required dataset to the back-end, thus simplifying the client's job to a single request (and removing almost all the extra time due to network latency). Figure 8-2 shows you how the change affected their back-end.

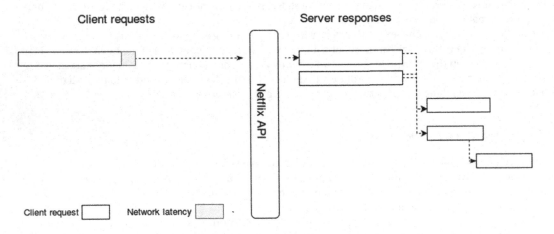

Figure 8-2. *New architecture with less client requests*

Now all important logic regarding gathering of information and how to put it all together has been moved back to the API's code, reducing all five requests from Figure 8-1 into a single one, essentially reducing the network latency costs of the entire process to that of a single request.

As a part of the change, and in order to truly achieve performance gains, they also decided to embrace concurrent programming while at the same time removing the inherently complex logic behind thread safety and parallel execution implementations from the client developer experience. Basically, they needed to give the developers hacking on their APIs a way to have all the power of concurrent programming without all the hustle that normally comes with it, and that was when they adopted reactive programming.

The Need for Concurrency

Concurrent execution on the back-end was crucial to get the performance gain they were looking for, because otherwise a single "big" client request would not really be able to compete against a bunch of "little" requests done by the same client using the old API mechanics, simply due to the fact that those little requests would all execute in parallel thanks to the concurrency provided by the Web server.

With this in mind, the good people at Netflix evaluated all their options (taking into account they were only dealing with Java). Callbacks and futures were not good enough; both techniques promised to get out of hand quickly if the logic got too complex.

But when they evaluated the reactive programming model, they realized it would give them the concurrency they needed and an easy-to-use and easy-to-understand model for the developers, which, in turn, would help, as I've said in the past, with development times. Improving time-to-market is, as you can probably guess, a big plus for most people.

If you think about it, the Reactive Model, by being push-based instead of pull-based, simplifies the task of concurrently getting the data from outside services and in a micro-services architecture, which would be the ideal case. The developer doesn't have to worry about threads or similar constructs, because the platform will take care of that, and getting the data from several sources at the same time is just a matter of subscribing to them and waiting for them to push it back.

To accomplish this, the developers at Netflix ported the RxJS library created by Microsoft (which I covered in Chapter 6) into the JVM creating RxJava (`https://github.com/ReactiveX/RxJava`). It can work with many of the languages that work on the JVM, like Scala, Groovy, and Clojure.

The Results

Netflix has reported on their tech blog that thanks to these changes, and the adoption of RP on the back-end, their developers have been able to successfully leverage concurrent programming without the typical problems that come with it.

The Case for Walmart

This case is actually specific to Walmart Canada, a subsidiary of Walmart and one of the largest retailers of the country. In this particular case, back in 2012, due to the ever-growing nature of Internet and the new devices that connect to it every day, their architecture started to fall short and traffic peaks started to affect them, leaving people out (see Figure 8-3 below for an example of such a case) of their online store and causing them to lose sales. Days like Black Friday (`https://en.wikipedia.org/wiki/Black_Friday_[shopping]`) and Cyber Monday (`https://en.wikipedia.org/wiki/Cyber_Monday`) were becoming a problem instead of an opportunity (see Figure 8-4 below for a chart of the traffic during peak days in 2012), so they had to act.

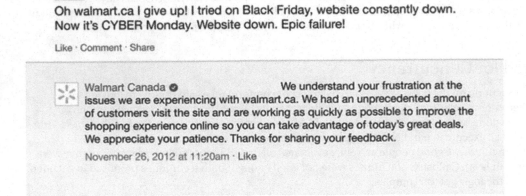

▶ Walmart Canada
November 26, 2012 · Medicine Hat

Oh walmart.ca I give up! I tried on Black Friday, website constantly down. Now it's CYBER Monday. Website down. Epic failure!

Like · Comment · Share

Walmart Canada ✔   We understand your frustration at the issues we are experiencing with walmart.ca. We had an unprecedented amount of customers visit the site and are working as quickly as possible to improve the shopping experience online so you can take advantage of today's great deals. We appreciate your patience. Thanks for sharing your feedback.

November 26, 2012 at 11:20am · Like

Figure 8-3. *Screenshot of a tweet regarding the status of Walmart's online capabilities in 2012*

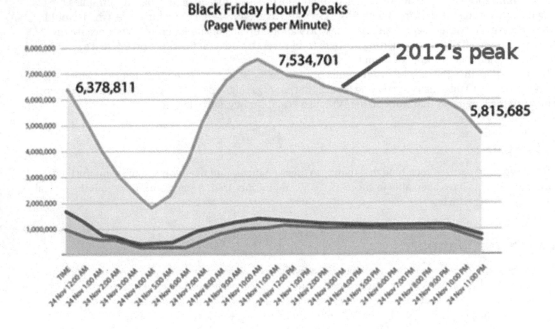

Figure 8-4. *Chart showing the increase in traffic during peak days*

Back then, their systems were based on Oracle ATG, which required a specialized group of developers, and the time to market was too high. Its ability to scale up was also very limited. All in all, they needed a change of perspective, and in order to scale up properly, they needed a new event-driven architecture.

The Proposed Solution

In order to achieve this, they needed to take a 180° turn, and so they started to research options, the winner turned out to be the Scala (`http://www.scala-lang.org/`), Akka (http://akka.io/), and Play (`https://www.playframework.com/`) combo. That technology stack runs on the JVM, so that provided a nice migration plan for the company, enabling them to ease the developers into the stack while doing the migration, instead of going all at once, with the corresponding trouble that approach can bring.

The Web framework (Play) would allow them to easily scale up and down their Web servers when needed. It would also help them leverage multi-core architectures and handle massively superior amounts of concurrent users than their old stack. Development times for the teams working on Play were between two and three times faster than those for the legacy teams.

With Scala and Akka, they were able to create a message-driven, reactive back-end architecture based on micro-services.

One of the advantages of going reactive was the simplification of the programming tasks; the improved time-to-market would allow them to bust out features much faster, just like the case with Netflix.

As it turns out, a reactive approach for a micro-services architecture, because with it you can translate the benefits of RP into your architecture, that is, it ends up being:

- *responsive*: meaning that the system will respond in a timely manner if possible.

- *resilient*: the system will stay responsive no matter what. Components are isolated form each other, providing containment in the face of failure.

- *message-driven*: the entire system relies on asynchronous message passing between components. This allows components to transmit failure as messages as well.

- *elastic*: the system will remain responsive under varying workloads.

The Results

In the next 4 weeks after these changes went live, Walmart.ca reported:

- An increase on conversions of 20%

- Their mobile orders went up by 98%

- A reduction of 36% on customer's page load time

- And, most importantly, **no downtime** during the peak traffic days like Black Friday

One More Case

As a final study case, instead of looking at another success case, let's build a little proof of concept ourselves, shall we? Using R-CheeseJS of course, I'm going to show you a pure Node.js app. It should provide, next to the code from the previous chapter, more practical insight into programming reactive systems.

The little PoC I'm going to build is a Chat app. It's going to be small, but it should be functional enough to make it interesting.

It'll have a server to centralize all communications and a client app that can be executed as many times as needed. Clients and server will communicate through sockets (I'll use socket.io, which can be found at `https://www.npmjs.com/package/socket.io`, to handle that code), and client-client communication will be done through the server.

A chat app is a great fit for a reactive approach, because there are a lot of opportunities to *react* to different events, such as incoming messages, users logging in and out, and even custom commands that can be sent from clients to the server. In this particular example, the app will:

- Allow any client to connect to the server and talk to the rest of the users.

- Every new login action will notify all connected clients of the event.

- Every client will be able to send messages that will be broadcast to all other clients.

- Each client can send a command to list all logged users in order to receive a list of all participants.

- Each client can send an exit command, effectively ending its connection to the chat server.

- Every time a client is disconnected, all other clients will be notified of that event.

- If the chat server is closed, all clients will handle that event gracefully.

The list of modules used for this example is minimal. I tried to keep it that way to show the power of the approach and, of course, the language itself:

- express.js (`https://www.npmjs.com/package/express`) is used to boot up the server, but nothing else.

- socket.io is used to create the chat server and handle all socket-related tasks.

- socket.io-client (`https://www.npmjs.com/package/socket.io-client`) provides the ability to create a command line client for socket.io instead of needing a Web browser (this app is 100% command line).

- Finally, winston (`https://www.npmjs.com/package/winston`) is used to simplify logging and message formatting on the console.

■ **Note** The other dependency that's not listed in there is the library shown on the previous chapter: rCheese.

Figure 8-5 shows a screenshot of the output from using the chat server (top section of the screen) with two clients (lower section of the screen). Let's look at the code now to understand how this can be implemented using rCheese in Node.js.

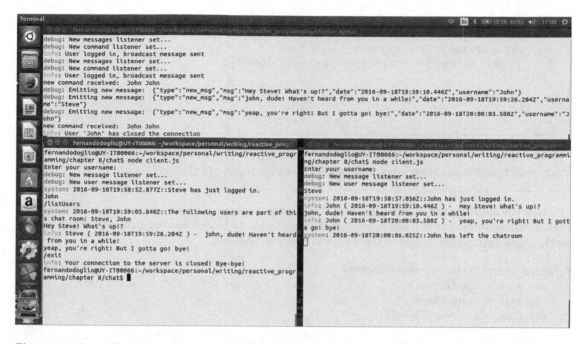

Figure 8-5. *Screenshot of two clients and the chat server interacting*

The Server

According to the list of features from before, the chat server can use four streams: one to handle the login action, another one to handle the new messages received, a third to handle the commands received by the clients.

And there is one final stream added to handle the exit command. Since it requires a few steps, let's see the code now:

■ **Note** As you are about to see, when transmitting objects through the Cheese streams, they need to be serialized and de-serialized. This is due to the fact that the internal stream used by the module is not set to be on object mode, so everything has to be a String.

The entry point for the server is this:

```
var app = require('express')();
var http = require('http').Server(app);
var io = require('socket.io')(http);
var rCheese = require("../cheese");
var logger = require("./logger");
var Cheese = rCheese.Cheese;

var map    = rCheese.Utils.map,
    filter = rCheese.Utils.filter;
```

```
io.on('connection', function(socket){
    socket.on('login', function(data) {
        var username = data.username;
        _USERS[username] = setupStreams(username, socket);
    });
});
```

■ **Note**   Although I will be using Winston to handle all logging needs, I'm creating a custom logger to handle colors and different logger levels, so all that code will be on the `logger.js` file.

Next you have the `setupStreams` function, which as you might've guessed, will set up the three main streams for every new user that logs in to the chat server. This is the largest function in the entire app, and that is simply because the flow for all three streams is determined here:

```
function setupStreams(usrname, socket) {
    var msgs = new Cheese();
    var logins = new Cheese();
    var commands = new Cheese();

    var msgsListener = false;
    var cmdListener = false;

    //== New messages stream
    //It simply broadcasts all messages sent if they have the required attributes
    msgs.fromFn(function(push) {
        if(!msgsListener) {
            msgsListener = true;
            logger.debug("New messages listener set...");
            socket.on('new_msg', function(msg) {
                if(msg.username == usrname) {
                    push(JSON.stringify(msg)); //serialize object
                }
            });
        }
    })
    .then(filter(function(m, done) {
        var mObj = JSON.parse(m.toString());
        done(null, mObj.msg != '' && mObj.msg != null && mObj.date != null && mObj.username
        != null);
    }))
    .each(function(obj) {
        //de-serialize object
        logger.debug("Emitting new message: ", obj.toString());
        socket.broadcast.emit('new_msg', JSON.parse(obj.toString()));
    });
```

130

```
    //== Commands stream
    commands.fromFn(function(push) {
        if(!cmdListener) {
            cmdListener = true;
            logger.debug("New command listener set...");
            socket.on('new_cmd', function(cmd) {
                console.log("new command received: ", cmd.username, usrname);
                if(cmd.username == usrname) {
                    push(JSON.stringify(cmd));
                }
            })
        }
    })
    .then(executeCommand)
    .then(filter(function(v, done) {
        done(null, v != null);
    }))
    .onError(function(err) { //format error message so it can be sent back to the client
        return JSON.stringify({msg: err.message, date: new Date()});
    })
    .each(sendBackResponse(socket));

    //== Login stream
    logins.fromArray([usrname])
    .then(map(function(username, done) { //turn the username into a message to send to
      everyone else
        var newObj = JSON.stringify({msg: [username, 'has just logged in.'].join(' '), date:
          new Date()});
        done(null, newObj);
    }))
    .each(function(obj) {
        logger.info("User logged in, broadcast message sent");
        socket.broadcast.emit('system_msg', JSON.parse(obj.toString()));
    });

  return {
    socket: socket,
    msgs: msgs,
    logins: logins,
    commands: commands
  };
}
```

As you can appreciate, the three first streams are there: logins, commands, and msgs. For commands and msgs I use the same technique to push data into them, and I set up a listener for the socket's correct event. Those listeners need a logic check to only be set once, because, as you might (or might not) remember, the function passed to fromFn is queried every few milliseconds. The first stream created is the one for the new messages that arrive from the clients, it is meant to only receive the event and broadcast it to all clients, but because it's so easy, I also added a previous validation step, filtering out messages that don't have the required fields.

The commands stream is also quite simple: Get the command object, execute it, and, if the command returns an object, then send it back to the client; otherwise, simply filter it out. You'll see the code for two commands below. One of them returns a response that needs to be sent back, and the other ones don't. This stream also handles errors, specifically the "Unknown command" error, which is a pretty easy one to cause.

Finally, the logins stream is created to handle the client's login message, which is the one that triggers this function's call, so instead of going with a socket listener, I'm using the fromArray method, passing in an array with only one item, the data received as part of the login event. This stream will process the event and be terminated afterward. One could argue the benefits of using a stream for such a case, but even though there is no need for reactive code for a single event, the code and the logic are clean and simple to understand, so I'd say it is worth it.

Let me now show you the last relevant bit of the server's code: the commands.

```
function executeCommand(cmd) {
    var cmdObj = JSON.parse(cmd.toString());

    var commands = {
        listUsers: listUsersCommand,
        exit: closeConnection
    };

    if(!commands[cmdObj.cmd]) {
        throw new Error("Error: Unknown command");
    } else {
        var result = commands[cmdObj.cmd](cmdObj);
        return (result !== null) ? JSON.stringify(result) : null;
    }
}
```

The preceding function, which triggers the execution of all commands, is actually quite simple. As you can see only two commands are supported, otherwise an error is thrown (which is caught by the rCheese module).

The EXIT command is the first and most complex of the two of them. The logic behind it can be split into several steps:

- Notify all users about the one that's leaving the chat room.

- End the connection between client and server.

- Remove the user from the in-memory list of connected users.

- Finally, print out a log message on the server console.

Now, following everything I've shown you so far about declarative programming, I took those four steps and turned them into a stream of, yet again, one single event:

```
//EXIT command main function
function closeConnection(cmd) {
    var exitStream = new Cheese();
    exitStream
        .fromArray([JSON.stringify(cmd)])
        .then(notifyUsers)
        .then(disconnect)
        .then(removeUser)
```

```
        .each(function(obj) {
            obj = JSON.parse(obj.toString());
            logger.info("User '" + obj.username + "' has closed the connection");
        });

    return null;
}


//Notify all users that one has left the chat room
function notifyUsers(cmd) {
    var cmdObj = JSON.parse(cmd.toString());
    var socket = _USERS[cmdObj.username].socket;
    if(!socket) throw new Error("Socket not found for user: ", cmdObj.username);

    socket.broadcast.emit('system_msg', {
        msg: [cmdObj.username, 'has left the chatroom'].join(" "),
        date: new Date()
    });
    return cmd;
}


//Close the connection between the client that wants to leave and the server
function disconnect(cmd) {
    var cmdObj = JSON.parse(cmd.toString());
    var socket = _USERS[cmdObj.username].socket;
    if(!socket) throw new Error("Socket not found for user: ", cmdObj.username);
    socket.disconnect();
    return cmd;
}


//Remove the user from the list of connected users and release its memory
function removeUser(cmd) {
    var cmdObj = JSON.parse(cmd.toString());
    delete _USERS[cmdObj.username];
    return cmd;
}
```

The helper functions here are all quite small, both in number of lines and logical complexity. They take care of doing one thing and nothing else, so all in all, the cognitive load (to use a term mentioned in a previous chapter) is quite low. Simply read the list of steps and get a function for each one. You can move them around or add new ones. It's as simple as changing the flow of the main stream and nothing more.

Finally, the other supported command, the list of connected users, is very easy to understand, since it boils down to a very simple function. The main difference between this one and the previous one is not its complexity, but its result. The exit command does a lot of things, but it does not send anything back to the client. But this one, all it does is send data back to the client. If you go up and look at the code for the command stream, you'll see that the filter step will let this one pass, and it will eventually end up being sent back through the socket connection.

```
///=== List Users command helper function
function listUsersCommand(cmd) {
    return {
        msg: ["The following users are part of this chat room:", Object.keys(_USERS).join(", ")].
            join(" "),
        date: new Date()
    };
}
```

The Client

The client application for this example will also be quite simple, it will allow users to log into the chat room, send messages and commands, and also receive messages from the server, system messages if you will, with error notifications, command responses, etc.—basically anything that's not from any client.

To achieve that description, I'm using three streams this time. One will handle the user input, which will translate into messages and commands sent to the server. Then one will handle the system messages and one will handle the messages sent by other users.

The input stream is interesting, because in Node.js, the standard input is represented as a stream, so you can create a Cheese stream from it, greatly simplifying the gathering of input from the user (which can be a bit of a complication). Here's the code for that:

client.js

```
var rChees  = require("../cheese");
var Cheese  = rChees.Cheese;
var Utils   = rChees.Utils;
var logger  = require("./logger");

var map      = Utils.map,
    reduce   = Utils.reduce,
    takeUntil = Utils.takeUntil,
    take     = Utils.take

var socket = require('socket.io-client')('http://localhost:3000');

var _USERNAME = null;

process.stdin.resume();
process.stdin.setEncoding('utf8');
var userLoggedIn = false;

var input = new Cheese(); //grabs user input from stdin
console.log("Enter your username: ");

socket.on('connect', function(){
    input
        .fromStream(process.stdin)
        .then(trim)
        .then(map(toObject))
        .onError(function(err) {
            console.trace("ERROR:" , err)
        })
        .each(send);
});
```

Basically, after connecting to the chat server, you immediately start listening for stdin events, which, luckly for us, are triggered when the ENTER key is pressed. So every data chunk received by this stream is a line the user entered. After that you trim it, turn it into an object with a format the chat server will recognize, and send it over. The toObject function is also one of the interesting ones, since that one takes care of sending the right data over, it could be a simple message, a command, or even the login action's input being sent over the wire.

```
///Helper functions
function printMessage(type) {
    if(!type) type = 'info';
    return function(str) {
        logger[type](str.toString());
    }
}

function send(str) {
    var msgObj = MsgParser(JSON.parse(str.toString()), socket)
    msgObj.send();
}

function toObject(str, done) {
    str = str.toString();
    var obj = null;

    if(_USERNAME) {
        obj = createMsgObj(str, _USERNAME)
    } else {
        obj = createLoginObj(str);
    }

    done(null, JSON.stringify(obj));
}

function newCommand(str, username) {
    var parts = str.split(" ");
    return {
        type: 'new_cmd',
        cmd: parts[0].replace("/", ""),
        args: parts.slice(1),
        username: username,
        date: new Date()
    };
}

function createMsgObj(inputStr, username) {
    if(inputStr.charAt(0) == '/') {
        return newCommand(inputStr, username);
    } else {
        return {
            type: 'new_msg',
            msg: inputStr,
```

```
            date: new Date(),
            username: username
        };
    }
}

function createLoginObj(newUserName) {
    _USERNAME = newUserName;
    return {
        type: 'login',
        username: newUserName,
        date: new Date()
    };
}

/*
Add a method to the JSON, so it knows how to send itself over the socket connection
*/
function MsgParser(msgObj, socket) {
    msgObj.send = function() {
        socket.emit(msgObj.type, msgObj);
    };
    return msgObj;
}

function trim(str) {
    return str.toString().trim();
}
```

Again, a set of small functions that take care of very specific tasks makes it very easy to modify and extend if needed.

The other two streams (system messages and user messages) are quite similar. They differ on the way they format the data and the way they print it out. Check it out:

```
var newMsgListener = false;
var newUserMsgListener = false;
var rcvdSystemMsgs = new Cheese(); //stream to grab system notifications
var userMsgs = new Cheese(); //stream to grab messages from other users

rcvdSystemMsgs
    .fromFn(newSystemMessage)
    .then(map(function(msg, done) {
        msg = JSON.parse(msg.toString());
        done(null, [msg.date, msg.msg].join('::'));
    }))
    .each(printMessage('system'));

userMsgs
    .fromFn(newUserMessage)
    .then(map(function(msg, done) {
        msg = JSON.parse(msg.toString());
```

```
        done(null, [msg.username, "(", msg.date, ") - ", msg.msg].join(' '));
    }))
    .each(printMessage());

function newSystemMessage(push) {
    if(!newMsgListener) {
        logger.debug("New message listener set...")
        socket.on('system_msg', function(sm) {
            push(JSON.stringify(sm));
        });
        newMsgListener = true;
    }
}

function newUserMessage(push) {
    if(!newUserMsgListener) {
        logger.debug("New user message listener set...")
        socket.on('new_msg', function(sm) {
            push(JSON.stringify(sm));
        });
        newUserMsgListener = true;
    }
}
```

As you can see on the preceding code, there is nothing really strange about it. Getting the events into each stream is done using a listener function, just like in the server code, and each stream only formats the data and prints them out in the right way. That's it!

To handle disconnect events, the following code is in place. It simply prints out a message and closes the application:

```
socket.on('disconnect', function(){
    logger.info("Your connection to the server is closed! Bye-bye!");
    process.exit(0);
});
```

Summary

Well, you're almost done with the book, just one more chapter left to go! With this chapter, you've learned not only that socket-based reactive code is possible and looks great but also that big companies are moving away from the more traditional programming paradigms and into the reactive one. This allows them to improve their dev time, essentially lowering their time-to-market, and it provides them with the tools required to create easy-to-maintain, scalable systems.

In the next and final chapter, I'm going to cover the basics of how to structure the reactive architecture of your systems, mixed with some tips that will come in handy when trying to scale up a Node.js application.

■ ■ ■

CHAPTER 9

Scaling Your Reactively Programmed Systems

Congrats! You made it to the final chapter of the book! So far you've received all the necessary information to add functional reactive logic on your Node.js applications, but the truth is, all of the examples I've showed you so far have been simplified to make them fit into the book in a format that would not bore you to death if you wanted to actually read the code. Real world applications, the ones that are actually out in production, ready for the end-users to access it, need to take other things into consideration. In some cases when the expected number of users is ever-growing, they need to be able to scale up to address the increasing demand.

Scaling up a Node.js application is actually quite simple, especially if you plan for it in advance and structure your system's architecture properly. In this chapter, I'm going to cover some of the basics behind scaling Node.js applications and specially, reactive systems written in Node.js. So, stay tuned and enjoy the final chapter of the book!

Scaling Node.js

The single-threaded architecture of Node.js sometimes tends to confuse people into thinking that it can't really scale up inside one single server. But the truth is, that in fact, that single-threaded model simplifies the task of scaling inside a single server, let's look into that shall we?

■ **Note**   Scaling up into several servers is quite simple as well, but it is not dependent on the threading model. Instead, it depends on the architectural decisions you take. I'll talk about those in a minute too.

Scaling Inside Your Server

The first stage when it comes to scaling, takes place inside the server, your single-threaded application, if executed normally (meaning, without the help of any external program, only with the default Node interpreter) then no matter how powerful your processor is, and how many cores it has, you're only using one of them.

I know right! Shocker, but by default, you're not taking full advantage of whatever beast you have for a processor. Fear not though! There are two seemingly different ways to accomplish this, and it all depends on what kind of application you're dealing with. I say "seemingly" though, because at the core of both of them, we're dealing with the same thing: processes.

© Fernando Doglio 2016
F. Doglio, *Reactive Programming with Node.js*, DOI 10.1007/978-1-4842-2152-5_9

Basically, in order to scale on multi-core processor computers, you need multiple processes, that's it. If you're dealing with your basic calculation intensive app, you'll probably want to spread said calculation between different workers, which basically are processes working in parallel and communicating with each other through some kind of protocol (I'll talk more about this further down the chapter, don't worry).

If, on the other hand, you have your basic webservice application, and you want to make sure those services are getting the power of the entire processor, then you can use the cluster(https://nodejs.org/api/cluster.html) module, which comes included with your Node.js installation. This module allows you to easily create copies of your application to run in parallel, each one on a different CPU core. Here's all the code you'll need to do just that:

```
var cluster = require('cluster');
var http = require('http');
var numCPUs = require('os').cpus().length;

if (cluster.isMaster) {
  // Fork workers.
  for (var i = 0; i < numCPUs; i++) {
    cluster.fork();
  }

  cluster.on('exit', function (worker, code, signal) {
    console.log("Worker",worker.process.pid, "died");
  });
} else {
  http.createServer(function(req, res){
    res.writeHead(200);
    res.end('hello world\n');
    process.exit(0);
  }).listen(8000, function() {
    console.log("Server Ready!")
  });
}
```

If you execute that code, once all servers are up and running, you'll see as many copies of the message *"Server Ready!"* as CPU cores you have. And if you visit your localhost at port 8000, you'll see on the console, how some of the workers start to die every time you hit the refresh button.

■ **Note** Even though the preceding code makes sure to only spawn as many processes as cores are on your CPU, you can change that number to anything you need. Set it high enough though, and you'll start getting negative performance results of course.

One of the main take-aways from the code shown before, aside from the simplicity of it, is that because workers can share TCP connections, you only need to code one single server, with no special considerations to the multiple instances you'll have running, and the simply start spawning new workers. You could potentially turn your already coded API into a multi-process application with the preceding code, and it would all still work!

All worker processes are handled by the main process (their parent), and that's the one that takes care of distributing the workload between all of them. In all operating systems (except for Windows) the default way of doing that is by distributing the load in a round robin fashion. In the case of Windows, the balancing is left to the Operating System.

Using an External Tool to Handle your Clustering Needs

The solution I showed before works, you can try it out and see the results, but if you go with it for your system, you might start to notice you're having to manually tackle some issues, like:

- Restarting dead workers. If for some reason, your workers start to crash, the cluster module will not take care of restarting them for you, you'll have to handle those particular cases by yourself.

- Elastic scaling. This is a particular interesting one, especially when you're running on pay-as-you-use servers, like Amazon's. How can you optimize the amount of workers based on your needs?

- What about monitoring? Checking the state of your workers is also something you don't get out of the box with the default module, but it might be something you need on a production environment.

So to answer the listed needs and more, you can use external tools that simplify the clustering process, in particular, I'm going to briefly go over one such tool called PM2 (http://pm2.keymetrics.io/).

First things first, the main benefit from PM2 is that you don't need *any* code added to your already existing app in order to make it work with multiple copies of the same process. Yes, the example from before showed that very little code is indeed needed, but even so, the added benefits of PM2 make it worth your while as well. So, to install it, you simply do:

```
$ npm install pm2 -g
```

And to start up your application with four instances in parallel, just use the following command:

```
$ pm2 start app.js -i 4
```

■ **Tip**   If you want to be sure PM2 starts as many workers as cores on your CPU, simply change that 4 with a 0.

Figure 9-1 shows the output from PM2 after starting a simple webserver script, with 0 instances, in my case, my processor has 4 cores, so I have 4 processes listed. The columns on the table are quite self explanatory, the *watching* column indicates whether the process will be restarted or not when a file changes and in order to enable it, you have to pass in the --*watch* flag.

```
[PM2] Spawning PM2 daemon with pm2_home=/home/fernandodoglio/.pm2
[PM2] PM2 Successfully daemonized
[PM2] Starting /home/fernandodoglio/workspace/personal/writing/reactive_programming/chapter 9/webserver.js in cluster_mode (0 instance)
[PM2] Done.
```

App name	id	mode	pid	status	restart	uptime	cpu	mem	watching
webserver	0	cluster	20521	online	0	0s	53%	23.6 MB	disabled
webserver	1	cluster	20530	online	0	0s	86%	23.9 MB	disabled
webserver	2	cluster	20547	online	0	0s	86%	21.6 MB	disabled
webserver	3	cluster	20567	online	0	0s	70%	17.8 MB	disabled

Use `pm2 show <id|name>` to get more details about an app

Figure 9-1. PM2 after being started

Now asides from the nice list of processes, you can rest assured, that if one of them is killed, PM2 will take care of restarting it, so accidental crashes will not stick.

You can also restart the entire cluster manually, with the restart command:

```
$ pm2 restart all
```

And, more interestingly, you can grow and shrink your cluster dynamically with the scale command. Passing in a number will scale (up or down) your cluster to have that many processes, prefixing the number with a + sign, will add that many processes:

```
$ pm2 scale webserver +3 #add 3 processes to the clustering
```

```
$ pm2 scale webserver 1 #downsize the cluster to only 1 process
```

Finally, one last, very nice gem, one that can help you update your code on production environments. You see, PM2 enables you to update your code without any downtime. It does it by restarting the processes one by one, and waiting for one to be fully up before restarting the next one, that way the cluster updates itself gradually. For this you can either use the reload command or the gracefulReload one, which instead of forcefully killing the cluster processes, it sends a shutdown signal allowing the process to gracefully do so.

```
$ pm2 reload webservice #kills the processes forcefully
```

```
$ pm2 gracefulReload webservice #sends a shutdown signal to them
```

You can catch the signal with the following block of code, and do whatever you need then:

```
process.on('message', function(msg) {
  if (msg === 'shutdown') {
    close_all_connections();
    delete_cache();
    server.close();
    process.exit(0);
  }
});
```

As you can see, PM2 can be a very handy tool to have on your... production belt, if you will, it packs a very big punch full of useful features and it's super easy to use. But then again, it's not like it's your clustering silver bullet (there is no such a thing by the way, never), you'll eventually run into some cases where classic clustering does not solve your problems, so what do you then? Let's find out!

What About Multiprocessing Without Clustering?

So what happens when the cluster module is not enough? What happens when the solution is not that simple? Like I mentioned before, multiprocessing is still the answer, make no mistake, if you want to get the most out of your processor, you'll need to work on splitting up your logic into several Node.js processes that can run in parallel, that will ensure you're using all cores.

Basically you go for a microservices approach, splitting your logic into smaller pieces that can work in parallel, so in other words, the more your business logic allows you to parallelize it's tasks, the more you'll be able make out of the architecture.

The upside to this approach, is that if your server starts to fall short , you can always migrate to a multi-server architecture with minor effort, because the code structure stays basically the same, you only need to handle the inter-server communication (dealing with networking issues like firewalls, enabling the right ports, and so on).

As you can probably imagine, there is no magic recipe for this particular scenario, you simply figure out a way to map your logic into a set of parallel processes (let's call them workers from now one, since that's what they'll be doing anyways), and if you can have several copies of each worker, even better. Now, normally, for this type of setups, the crucial part is not how you spawn new workers, but how you handle the communication between them, because you'll most like want them to send data between different types of workers and eventually save that data (the final output) someplace you can use it. And here is were we talk a bit about the best options for IPC (Inter-Process-Communication in Node.js).

IPC in High Performance Land

There are almost too many options when it comes to picking the right way of doing IPC in Node.js, but thanks to the fact that in this chapter, I'm dealing with highly scalable and performant architectures, the options for doing efficient IPC are narrowed considerably for us. You see, most IPC modules out there, deal with direct process-to-process communication, some even rely on the assumption that the processes will always share the same server and as I've stated already, that might not always be the case, in fact, if you're truly dealing with a scalable solution, you should have this down as a basic assumption: you'll need several servers to handle your different workers.

So, if direct process-to-process communication is off the table, then what are our options? In my experience, using a scalable solution to act as a data buffer to distribute the load between the different instances of the same worker type, is the right way to go, because:

1. It allows for processes to transfer data between them at the rate they choose (you can either choose to throttle it, or simply go as fast as you have workers available).

2. The buffer solution can scale on its own, thus removing the need for you to worry about it, simply configure your buffer to scale and watch it go (more or less, but you get my point, you don't have to worry about things like sharding of the data, availability, etc).

Figure 9-2 shows a generic example of what I described before, on it, you have represented three different types of workers, their types indicate their main tasks, so each task can be parallelized and that is also represented on the diagram as multiple instances of the same worker type. The communication between types is done using some external solution as data buffers, just like I mentioned as well. So in the future, if you're correctly measuring the performance of the system, you can detect which parts of it as under stress and adjust accordingly. Say you get overwhelmed by client requests, you can simply scale on the "type A" workers, the rest of the system will simply continue to process the data as fast as it can, unless of course your "type A" workers are generating too much data for the "Data Buffer #1", in such a case, you can scale up that buffer and the rest of the process continues the same. See the pattern? Scaling up became super easy from an architectural standpoint, you simply need more instances, and finally, if your servers start to become overwhelmed by the number of instances, again, you can simply add more servers and spread the workers throughout the cluster.

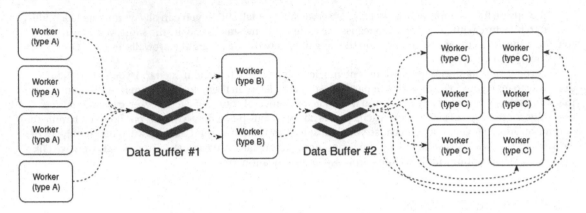

Figure 9-2. *Basic example of a multi-worker communication using data buffers*

Figure 9-3 shows how the sample architecture would look like once you've scaled up your "type A" workers and you "Data Buffer #1", like I said, the rest of it is unaffected.

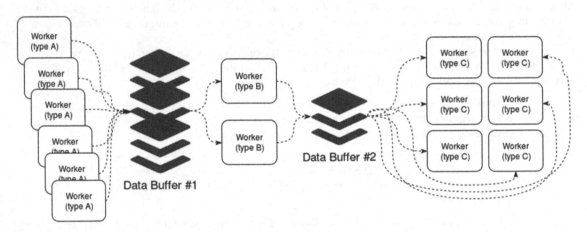

Figure 9-3. *The scaled up version of the previous architecture*

Let's look at some choices of technologies for the data buffers, there are many names out there that can do pretty much the same, so lets group them into two different categories: push based buffers, and pull based buffers.

Push Based Buffers

Or in other words, buffers that will push the new data to your workers as soon as it becomes available. For this type of buffers, Message Queues are a great options, by default most queues work this way. In this model, you have three basic actors:

- A publisher, which takes care of sending the data into the queue and then forgets about it.

- A subscriber, which registers itself into the queue for a specific type of message and then waits for them.

- The actual queue, which receives the messages from the publisher and relays them to the first subscriber available.

- The advantages of this approach are:

- The publishers only need to know how to send the data to the queue, then they can forget about it. This simplifies the job of the developer working on this process, since they don't need to worry about retries, lack of consumers, storage for the messages, etc.

- Consumers also benefit from the simpler logic that comes with this approach, since they only need register on the queue and then simply wait for it to push a message to them.

- Finally, the queue itself is the one that takes most of the hit, it needs to handle the messages in, and the messages out, it needs to handle scalability, temp storage for the messages in case of failure, and many other aspects of being a functional scalable queue. That being said, the great thing about this, is that that's all taken care of, unless you're coding your own message queue, you're most likely using one of the common ones, Apache Kafka (http://kafka.apache.org/), RabbitMQ (https://www.rabbitmq.com), Redis' Pub/Sub (http://redis.io/) to name just a few.

Depending on your particular needs, you might want to go with one or the other, for instance, if you're dealing with a huge incoming traffic (say 100k requests / second) you might want to go with Kafka, if on the other hand, you have complex routing logic for messages, you might want to consider going with RabbitMQ. So you see, even though the approach is the same on all of them (and I just named three options), they're not all exactly the same, so reading up on the major options out there might be a good idea.

Just to illustrate how easy it can be to interact with one of these queues, here is a simple example of a publisher and a consumer (subscriber) that work with RabbitMQ, this example is using the module amqp (https://www.npmjs.com/package/amqp):

```
// == CONSUMER CODE ==
var amqp = require('amqp');

var connection = amqp.createConnection({ host: 'localhost' });

// add this for better debuging
connection.on('error', function(e) {
  console.log("Error from amqp: ", e);
});

// Wait for connection to become established.
connection.on('ready', function () {
  console.log("Listening for messages...");
  connection.queue('my-queue', function (q) {
      // Catch all messages
      q.bind('#');

      // Receive messages
      q.subscribe(function (message) {
        // Print messages to stdout
        console.log(message.data.toString());
      });
  });
});
```

```
//== PUBLISHER CODE ==
var amqp = require('amqp');

var connection = amqp.createConnection({ host: 'localhost' });

// add this for better debuging
connection.on('error', function(e) {
  console.log("Error from amqp: ", e);
});

// Wait for connection to become established.
connection.on('ready', function () {
  // Use the default 'amq.topic' exchange
  connection.publish('my-queue', 'Test message');
  console.log("Message sent!");
});
```

Nothing fancy, you can split the preceding code into two files, first execute the consumer so it can subscribe to Rabbit and then execute the publisher, it will send a message to the queue that will be received and printed by the consumer.

Pull Based Buffers

Given the benefits of the push strategy, why would we want to go with the opposite? Well, for starters, if you have too many consumers (how many are too many will depend on the queue you're using at the moment), the time it takes for the middleware (the actual queue) the notification process that takes place to let me them about the new message might take too long.

Also, this type of model is subject to problems with the rate of consumption from the subscribers is lower than the rate of productions of the publishers, in that case the buffer might run out of memory, or storage of suffer from kind of problem that might lead to a system-wide issue (think Denial of Service attack here).

If instead of giving the queue the responsibility of finding the one subscriber that can handle the new message, you get the consumers to query the queue on fixed time intervals and pull the messages out, then you remove that problem. Now, the queuing solution that you're using will be hit both, by the consumers and by the publishers, this translates into more traffic going in to it, so you'll have to take that into account when scaling.

Pulling also adds another layer of complexity to your consumers, because not only do they have to query the queue, they also need to handle race conditions raised when several consumers attempt to grab the same message. You only want one of them to actually process it, and the rest to move on to the next one.

Taking out a message from the queue, or marking it as read, or whatever technique you use to make sure only one consumer gets it, needs to be atomic, meaning, it needs to happen on a single instruction.

Even though the model for interacting with the queuing solution in this case is different, the actual products out there aren't that different. Most of the message queues out there support pull based operations, so Kafka, RabbitMQ, those are all still options, Redis' Pub/Sub for instance is not, it will not directly work, but you can easily work around it by using a list as your main queue, and setting lock keys for your messages, in order to mark them as read before taking them out of the queue.

So, Pull or Push?

As you might've guessed by now, there is no simple answer to this question, the type of model you choose will depend entirely on your use case. Hopefully both descriptions has given you enough information to pick, but just to recap:

You would normally go with a push based buffer when:

- You need to keep your logic simple.

- You don't have an enormous amount of consumers working in parallel.

- You're looking to react to it as soon as the messages arrive.

On the other hand, you would rather go with a pull based approach when:

- You are dealing with really high traffic into your system

- You want to have control over the rate of consumption of your messages

- You want to process the messages in batches, instead of one by one as they come

Creating Reactive Systems

Over these nine chapters, I've covered what Reactive Programming means, I've shown examples, even created a library that allowed you to do some reactive programming yourself, but when it comes to architectural decisions, there are a set of considerations that you can have if you want to create reactive systems.

In this last section of the chapter, I'm going to cover those considerations. Reactive systems are meant to be more flexible, loosely coupled and easily scalable (we already covered some of it before in the chapter). Essentially making these systems easier to develop, more fault tolerant and able to gracefully react to errors. And to accomplish this, your systems need to meet the following criteria:

Responsive Systems

Reactive systems need to be responsive, meaning, they need to **always** provide feedback to the users and they need to do so in a timely manner, a consistent response time is a requirement for these systems. In turn it will provide a better user experience and better error handling.

In order to achieve this, as you'll see, the system needs to comply with the requirements listed below, since it needs to be resilient in order to always be responsive, it needs to be elastic, in order to always provide a response back to the end user in a timely manner and it needs to be message driven to do so, because as you probably know by now, elastic scaling comes mainly from micro-service based architectures, and in order to communicate those services with each other you'll need some kind of message system.

Resilient to Errors

Reactive systems are supposed to be resilient to all errors. That doesn't mean your system is 100% error free, instead, it means it can handle unexpected errors gracefully, instead of crashing uncontrollably. This in turn, helps ensure the previous requirement, since any system that is not resilient will eventually become unresponsive at one point or another.

Achieving an architecture that is resilient and capable of handling all sorts of errors and crashes is not simple, in fact several areas need to be taken into account, for instance:

- Replication, to ensure redundancy, both of the data and the services. Data stores are a good example in this case, they normally provide a cluster mode, which not only provides data redundancy but also add back-up server for every active master to ensure the service is always working by avoiding single points of failure on their architectures.

- Containment and isolation to make sure failure on one component stays independent of the rest of the system, it prevents a fatal cascading effect where one simple error or unhandled exception crashes a system, which in turn crashes another and so on until the entire architecture is unresponsive.

- And delegation, making sure all components can delegate responsibilities between each other (like error handling, logging, and so on).

Elastic Scaling

Elasticity on a system is usually intended to reference it's capacity to handle varying amounts of load by increasing or decreasing the resources used. During the first section of this chapter, this topic was covered and examples were given on how to design architectures that are able to scale up or down when needed and still remain functional.

Depending on your infrastructure, the tools used to measure and handled the elasticity may vary, usually cloud providers like Amazon and Microsoft's Azure provide you with the tools to automate such processes, but there are always tools you can use to manually perform these tasks.

The point of this requirement is, simply put, that a reactive system should be able to *react* to the current work load and adjust it's available resources accordingly to provide cost-effective performance, meaning, scaling down to save resources when they're not needed, as well as scaling up but only as much as needed, to keep the costs of such resources under a certain pre-set roof.

Message Driven

Finally, reactive systems should have their components communicate using asynchronous messages, allowing for most of the requirements I've listed. This even allows for errors to be treated as messages that can be sent from one component to the other.

As I stated before, this single requirement is the corner stone for all of the others, this mechanism provides the necessary foundation for all services to communicate with each other, which in turn provides the ability to keep scaling the number of processes without affecting their capacity to talk to each other, and which in turn, means your system is capable to coming up with a response and sending it back to the end-user in a short enough timespan.

All in all, as you can see, the title "Reactive systems" makes it sound a lot bigger than it actually is, in fact, the list of requirements is just a list of good design decisions that will help your architecture provide a good user experience and to react to both, the user's input and the changes on it's environment.

Summary

Scaling your applications with Node.js and having a look at some interesting architectural decisions that in turn, will help you create better systems was the final piece to the reactive puzzle that this book is. You've read it, you got it, now it's time for you to go and start applying what you (hopefully) learned into your code.

Just remember a few tips:

- Reactive and functional programing are a great match.

- When it comes to Node.js, reactive programming is almost all about streams, so don't fear them, embrace them and you'll love it!

- If you haven't yet, accept Node's asynchronous mentality, it will save you a lot of trouble.

- And finally, remember to properly design your system into components that you can parallelize and scale.

Finally, let me thank you for accompanying me throughout the book, I sincerely hope you've found it useful and interesting and that there is at least one thing you can take away from it, if that's the case, then my work is done.

Index

Get the eBook for only $4.99!

Why limit yourself?

Now you can take the weightless companion with you wherever you go and access your content on your PC, phone, tablet, or reader.

Since you've purchased this print book, we are happy to offer you the eBook for just $4.99.

Convenient and fully searchable, the PDF version enables you to easily find and copy code—or perform examples by quickly toggling between instructions and applications.

To learn more, go to http://www.apress.com/us/shop/companion or contact support@apress.com.

Printed in the United States
By Bookmasters